BONSAI
Nature
in Miniature

BONSAI
Nature in Miniature

Kyuzo Murata
&
Isamu Murata

SHUFUNOTOMO/JAPAN PUBLICATIONS

Book design by Office 21
Photographs by Shufunotomo Co., Ltd.
Edited by Michiko Kinoshita and Kate Gorringe-Smith

First printing, September, 2000

Published by Shufunotomo Co., Ltd.
2-9, Kanda Surugadai, Chiyoda-ku
Tokyo, 101-8911 Japan

DISTRIBUTORS
United States: Kodansha America, Inc., through Oxford University Press
198 Madison Avenue, New York, NY 10016.
Canada: Fitzhenry & Whiteside Ltd.
195 Allstate Parkway, Markham, Ontario L3R 4T8.
United Kingdom and Europe: Premier Book Marketing Ltd.
Clarendon House, 52, Cornmarket Street, Oxford, OX1 3HJ, England.
Australia and New Zealand: Bookwise International
54 Crittenden Road, Findon, South Australia 5023.
The Far East and Japan : Japan Publications Trading Co., Ltd.
1-2-1 Sarugaku-cho, Chiyoda-ku, Tokyo, 101-0064 Japan

ISBN 4-88996-060-0
Printed in China

PREFACE

The art of bonsai, together with that of ikebana or Japanese flower-arrangement, originated in Japan and is now admired throughout the world. Among the lovers and admirers of bonsai are many who find infinite pleasure in growing their own bonsai? The satisfaction of creating with their own hands the beauty of nature in miniature. Although there are several publications on bonsai, very few books have been published for beginners.

This book is designed to equip those who wish to embark upon growing their own bonsai with the knowledge and skills to do so. To this end, we have included as many photographs and illustrations as possible in the hope of giving the reader a complete and comprehensive explanation of the pleasurable and rewarding art of bonsai growing.

You will find outlined in this book every step, from the basics of how to choose a tree, what fertilizer to use and when to water, to the more skilled techniques such as wiring the branches of your tree into the desired shape. This book will be a practical help and welcome companion to all those who desire to grow bonsai, emphasizing both the growing techniques and the pleasures to be gained from viewing your plant as a work of art.

Bonsai changes with the seasons, so will give the grower enjoyment throughout the year—a pleasure that cannot be obtained from growing flowers in the garden. And, as it grows older, the more your bonsai will come to exhibit the beauty of its full-sized counterpart in nature. This is the pleasure that the authors wish to share with as many people as possible.

CONTENTS

FOUR SEASONS OF BONSAI

Wild cherry (*Prunus donarium* Sieb. var. *spontanea* Makino)
50 years old, 75 cm (30 inches), Yama-Zakura
Tokoname ware by Shōsen, drum shape
Sō-kan (twice-sprit trunk style)
This tree should be put where it will get plenty of sunlight and air. Twigs which grow too long should be nipped immediately, leaving only 2 or 3 buds near the base.

Wild cherry, weeping type (*Prunus donarium* Sieb. var. *spontanea* Makino)
70 years old, 60 cm (24 inches), Yama-Zakura
Bizen ware, round shape
Grows in mountains. A characteristic of this tree is that its leaves and flowers appear at the same time; the shape of its trunk is also naturally beautiful. It is a deciduous tree widely used as bonsai. The tree shown in the photograph is a grafted tree.

Flowering Japanese Quince (*Chaenomeles speciosa*
Nakai cv. 'Tōyōnishiki')
25 years old, 13 cm (4¹/₂ inches), Boke ('Tōyōnishiki')
Handmade container
Miniature bonsai (*komono* bonsai or *shōhin* bonsai)
A short, deciduous tree which originated in China. It
grows a profusion of beautiful flowers. Branches with
red flowers should be kept from growing too large;
branches with white flowers, however, should be
encouraged to grow, as these branches tend to grow
flowers with a mix of both red and white petals. By doing
this, a balance between both colors can be achieved.

Flowering Japanese Quince (*Chaenomeles speciosa*
Nakai cv. 'Tōyōnishiki')
70 years old, 45 cm (18 inches), Boke 'Tōyōnishiki'
Tokoname ware by Seizan, rectangular shape
Kabu-dachi (clumped trunk style)
Tōyōnishiki trees grow two types of flowers: those that
have a mixture of white and red petals, resembling a tie-
dye pattern, and those whose petals are either red or
white.

11

Wisteria (*Wistaria floribunda* (Wild.) DC.)
130 years old, total length: 100 cm (40 inches), Noda-Fuji
Tokoname ware, square shape
Kengai (cascade style)
A Noda-Fuji type tree. Known for the large number of tassel-like flowers it grows, these flowers can be purple, white or red. Purple flowers, however, are considered to be the most beautiful and elegant and have provided the inspiration for countless Japanese poems since ancient times. This precious bonsai was a gift from the family of Prince Arisugawa to Prince Takamatsu.

Wisteria (*Wistaria brachybotrys* Sieb. et Zucc.)
130 years old, left and right: 72 cm (29 inches), Yama-Fuji
Tokoname ware, square shape
Han-kengai (semi-cascade style)
A Yama-Fuji type tree. It has been grafted once. This tree grows in fertile and moist soil. As it is a climbing plant, it is best suited for cascade, semi-cascade and slanted-trunk styles. It needs plenty of water and fertilizer, so it must be given both not only during the growing periods of spring and fall, but also during its dormant period.

Kaidō Crab Apple (*Maulus halliana* Koehne)
80 years old, 50 cm (20 inches), Suishi Kaido
Tokoname ware by Shōsen, 'Fukuro'-style oval shape
Sō-kan (twice-split trunk style)
A short, deciduous tree indigenous to China. Its flowers
are dark-red, and its branches have a tendency to expand
and droop down.

Kishi Azalea (*Rhododendron ripense* Makino)
15 years old, 50 cm (20 inches), Kishi-Tsutsuji
Tokoname ware by Shōsen, round-shape
Yose-ue (group planting style)
This tree was taken from the Shimanto river in Shikoku;
it is indigenous to the mountains and river banks of
Shikoku. Its trunk is strong and straight. Its flowers are a
pure, lovely light purple.

Miyama-Kirishima Azalea
(*Rhododendron kiusianum* Makino)
40 years old, left and right: 84 cm (33½ inches), Miyama-Kirishima
Chinese 'Senkōyō' hexagonal container
Han-kengai (semi-cascade style)
Short evergreen, indigenous to the highlands of Kyūshū. Pairs of leaves grow alternately on each side of the branches. Its branches diverge into many more branches. The basic color of its flowers is a light purple, although there are many other variations of this tone. This tree has the appearance and characteristics typical of trees which grow in alpine areas.

Gardenia (*Gardenia jasminoides* Ellis var. *grandiflora* Makino)
20 years old, 22 cm (9 inches), Kuchinashi
Handmade container
Kabu-dachi (clumped trees style)
Short evergreen. Its lovely white flowers blossom in early summer and yield a pleasant fragrance. As this tree grows in warm climates, winter is its number one enemy. Although the tree in the illustration has thicker leaves and its leaves have rounder edges than the usual bonsai species—in addition to the fact that it has a characeristically straight trunk—its beautiful flowers make it an ideal choice for bonsai.

Hinoki Cypress (*Chamaecyparis obtusai* Sieb. et Zucc.)
20 years old, 26 cm (10 inches), Hinoki
Yose-ue (group planting style)
Tokoname ware, Rectangular shape
The hinoki cypress is a tree species often grown in
clumps (forest-style). It is environmentally adaptable
and easy to grow.

Hornbeam (*Carpinus laxiflora* Blume)
35 years old, 63 cm (25 inches), Aka-Shide
Yose-ue (group planting style)
Shigaraki ware, oval shape
Its small leaves are also pretty after turning yellow in
autumn. In Japan the Hornbeam has long been liked as
a clumped bonsai.

Morrow Honeysuckle (*Lonicera morrowii* A Gray)
80 years old, 66 cm (26 inches), Hyōtan-boku
Ban-kan (twisting trunk style)
Bizen ware, round shape
Deciduous shrub that flowers May through June. Pairs of flowers bloom in syndesis, with each flower producing two gourd-shaped fruit that are crimson in color and deadly poisonous. This shrub was brought down from the mountains and already naturally bent. Should be well fertilized and placed in a sunny position.

Saghalien Spruce (*Picea glehni* Mast.)
150 years old, approx. 75 cm (30 inches), Aka-Ezo-Matsu
Sha-kan (slanting trunk style), Tokoname ware by Shōsen, drum shape
Grows in the southern region of Saghalin. Evergreen. The trunk is growing almost perpendicular to the ground. This tree was taken from Kunashirito 70 years ago. Apart from growing a few small branches, the size of the trunk has remained basically the same. Although this tree comes from a cold region, it still needs to be protected from the cold dry winter winds. Since its trunk can be made to imitate that of the pine tree, the most representative of all bonsai trees, this tree is suitable to be grown in any of the straight trunk, slanted trunk, cascade trunk, group planting and rock grown bonsai styles.

Japanese Red Pine (*Pinuss densiflora* Sieb. et Zucc.)
100 years old, 106 cm (42 inches), Aka-Matsu
Sha-kan (slanting trunk style)
Tokoname ware, round shape
Because it is difficult to find a red pine with a thick trunk, this species is suited to forms such as the 'Bunjin-gi' style. Water sparingly, as too much water causes too much succulent growth.

Hime-Gaki 'Roa' persimmon (*Diospyros rhombifolia* Hemsl.)
15 years old, 37 cm (15 inches), Hime-Gaki
Kabu-dachi (clumped trees style)
Tokoname ware by Shōsen, oval shape
Native to China, it is a strong and fertile fruit-bearing shrub. It is considered ideal for bonsai. It grows mainly in the Chinese provinces of Fujian and Zhejiang.

Chestnut 'Issai-Guri' (*Castanea crenata* Sieb. et Zucc.)
30 years old, 74 cm (30 inches), Kuri 'Issai-Guri'
Bunjin-gi (literati style), Tokoname ware, Fukuro-style
One way to grow this tree is to start by planting a chestnut and raising the seedling in a smallish pot with little
fertilizers. This will eliminate the need to apply training
wire. Once the tree's framework is built, shape the tree by
trimming. Pruning can be accomplished sufficiently by
cutting the succulent sprouts.

Wild Persimmon (*Diosyros kaki* Thunb. var. *sylvestris* Makino)
70 years old, 70 cm (24 inches), Yama-Gaki
Kōra-buki ('turtle shell' style: The bottom part of the trunk looks like a turtle's shell)
Tokoname ware by Shōsen, drum-like shape
Tall, deciduous tree with small leaves. Its fruit is also small. Although the branches of the persimmon are fragile, and the tree is vulnerable to dry weather, its trunk is basically strong, which makes it easy for any bonsai enthusiast to grow. In addition, its fruit has a beautiful shape and stays on the tree for a long period of time, making the bonsai a pleasure to gaze at any time of the year.

Japanese Maple (*Acer palmatum* Thunb. var. *palmatum*)
30 years, 89 cm (35 1/2 inches), Iroha-Momiji
Bunjin-gi (literati style)
Tokoname ware, round shape
The natural shape of this tree's trunk had the characteristics of the literati (bunjin-gi)
style, so no effort was made to shape it into any other style. The trunk of this style of tree
should look fragile and ready to bend with the wind.

Sawara Cypress (*Wisteria Chamaecyparis pissifera* Endl.)
50 years old, 50 cm (20 inches), Hime-Sawara
Hōki-dachi (broom style)
Tokoname ware by Shōsen, drum-like style
Tall evergreen conifer. Its trunk is straight.

Japanese Bantam Cypress (*Chamaecyparis obtusa* Endl. var. *breviramea* Mast.)
100 years old, 81 cm (32¹/₂ inches), Chabo-Hiba
Moyō-gi (informal trunk style)
Tokoname ware by Seizan, oval shape
It belongs to the Japanese Cypress family. Its trunk is straight and its branches are short and grow parallel to the ground.
Its branches, in turn, diverge into many more little branches. These branches have a tendency to grow densely and over-
lap each other.

HOW TO TRANSPLANT BONSAI

(1) The photographs shows a 'Goyō-Matsu' (Five-Needled Pine) that has not been transplanted for 5 years. Transplanting should be done in spring when the temperature is almost 65°F (18°C). Slide tweezers down and around the inside of the pot to separate the roots from the sides.

(2) Lift the plant gently out of the container.

(3) Cut off about one third of the bottom with a long knife.

(4) Cut off about one third around the sides with a long knife.

(5), (6) Remove the old soil. Trim all overgrown roots.

(7), (8) Cover the drain holes at the bottom of the container with plastic net. Pass plastic string through the drain holes. Do not use any copper wire, as copper wire may rust and harm the roots.

(9) Insert two plastic strings through the roots horizontaly.

(10) Cover the hole at the bottom of the container, and put a small amount of soil at the bottom.
(11) Put the plant in and determine its position in the container. Put some soil around the roots. Fasten the tree in the container by inserting a plastic string.
(12) Put in all the soil making sure that the soil penetrates the fine roots. To ensure this use a stick or pencil.
(13) Lastly press the soil down lightly with a trowel or butter knife.

(14) After planting, water until it flows out of the hole at the bottom of the container. Place the container where it will only get morning sun. Be sure that it is not exposed to any strong winds. After two or three days, give water as you would to any other plant.

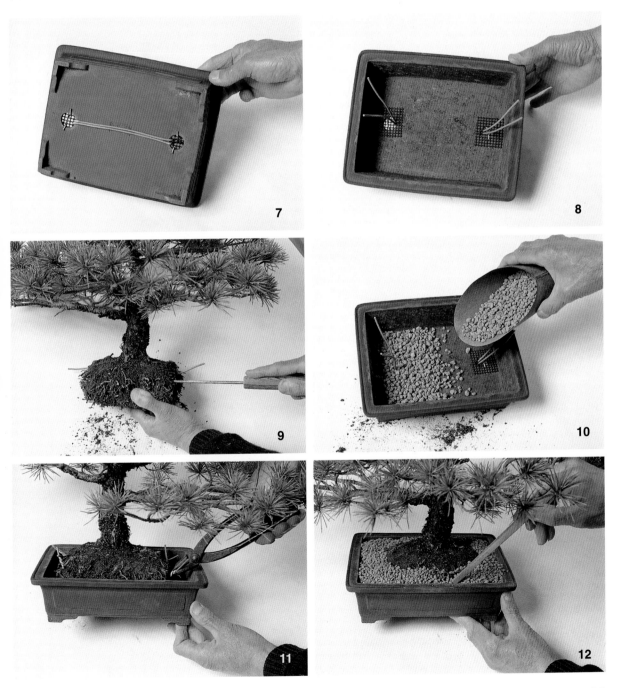

Five-Needled Pine (*Pinus pentaphylla Mayr* var. *himekomatsu* Makino)
40 years old, 30 cm (12 inches), Goyō-Matsu
Chokkan (formal straight style), Tokoname ware, oval shape
Evergreen tree. This is a recently transplanted bonsai. The five-needled pine is called such because its needles are in groups of five. This species needs little care, is robust, and has an upright trunk well suited to the 'Moyō-gi' style, in which the whole tree works to create pattern. It can assume a variety of shapes including the 'Bunjin-gi' style, cascade, and multiple-trunk growth.

I

Answer to questions concerning the art of bonsai

What is bonsai ?

Bonsai is the art of growing miniature trees, bushes, or perennial herbs in such a way as to capture the natural grandeur of an ancient tree, or the special character of a landscape. Bonsai was invented by the Japanese, a people famous for their love of gardening, and is considered in Japan to be the highest form of horticulture that the hobby gardener can practice.

In fact, the best examples of bonsai can only be fully appreciated if they are considered artworks in themselves, much like a painting or a sculpture. But even if you're not quite aiming for such heights, the pleasure of growing bonsai is unique, and its decorative purposes—both in the garden and indoors—make it an art that will yield lasting enjoyment.

What are the elements of bonsai?

Bonsai are made up of three elements: (1) the container in which the tree is planted; (2) the soil; and (3) the plant or group of plants which are grown in the container. Of these, the first two represent the earth, and the plants represent the herbs, bushes, and trees that grow on the earth. Rocks can be used as additional features to help create the feeling of a natural environment.

A primary consideration for the beginner is to choose a container and soil that will promote the healthy growth of the plant. When choosing a container, large containers are best avoided, as they require a great deal of soil which will make them cumbersome to handle, and they also tend to take up more space than is desirable. The most best container is one that you can easily move by yourself.

Plants that make good bonsai are those that can grow within a restricted space and still exhibit all the characteristics of the full-sized plant. The best plants are therefore those that come in dwarf varieties, or those that lend themselves to being grown as miniature plants.

What are the features of a true bonsai ?

A bonsai plant must exhibit the following features:
(1) It must have all the vitality of a living plant.
(2) It should capture the aged appearance of a full-sized tree that is several decades old. In addition, the tree as a whole, in its container, should recreate the landscape of a tree growing in a vast wood.
(3) The branches must vary in length and shape, and combine to create an artistic effect.
(4) The shape of the container and the appearance of the trees or herbs planted therein must be perfectly balanced, so that the overall effect is one of stability.
(5) The plants must exhibit all the variations that accompany the changes of the seasons, so that they give pleasure all year round.
(6) Since all bonsai growers value nature, the best plants to choose are those that will betray only a minimum of artificiality. It may therefore be preferable to enhance some of the tree's natural 'imperfections' than to force it into a more 'symmetrical' yet unnatural shape.

Sasa (Small Bamboo) and Aka-Ezo-Matsu (Saghalien Spruce) planted on a flat rock to represent a miniature natural landscape.

What are the points to look for in a good example of bonsai ?

The point of bonsai has always been the appreciation of the plant as a whole. However, when viewing bonsai, the following areas deserve attention as being particularly desirable:

(1) In the case of a single tree;

(a) The condition of the roots: it is a much sought sign of age and character if the roots of a bonsai have grown thick and sturdy and are visible above ground;

(b) The appearance of the trunk: the trunk must be thick and strong, particularly at its base;

(c) The curvature of the trunk; this should have a natural grace, as in an aged tree shaped by the elements;

Kuro-Matsu (Japanese Black Pine) grown to reproduce in miniature the appearance of a grand old tree.natural state.

Goyō-Matsu (Five-Needled Pine), a bonsai masterpiece with two trunks.

Keyaki (Zelkova), one of the famous trees of Keyaki bonsai.

combine to create an artistic, but not artificial, whole.

(b) Curvature of the branches: This should combine with the placement of the group to look natural and harmonious and create a sense of perspective.

(3) In the case of herbs:

(a) The distribution of the plants: these should have the feel of a cluster of plants in their natural environment.

(b) The condition of the blossoms and fruits, and their color arrangement: as above these should add greatly to the beauty of the plants individually and create a harmonious and natural effect as a group.

What kind of plants are suitable for bonsai?

Approximately 3,000 plant species or varieties are found in the territory of Japan, which extends from the subtropics to the subarctic zone. Of these, roughly half are suitable to be grown as bonsai. However, about 40% of the total vegetation is trees and, of these, nearly 80% can be grown as bonsai.

(d) The rugged appearance of the bark: this should create the illusion of great age;

(e) The artistic appearance of the branches: this should also recreate the illusion of great age;

(f) The appearance of the leaves: their shape and colour, as well as their changes from season to season, should add to the beauty of the plant and mimic the character of the full-sized plant.

(g) The blossoms and fruits: as with the foliage, these should combine, in all their variations of shape and colour, to enhance the beauty of the whole and to recreate the character of a full-sized tree.

(h) The direction of the top: the terminal, or topmost point of the tree, should incline forward slightly. This is a critical element of bonsai, as the terminal symbolizes the life that is inherent in the tree.

(i) The mosses that cover the soil: these should help create the illusion that the tree is growing in a miniature natural environment.

(2) In the case of trees and herbs planted together, in addition to the previous points:

(a) The girth and height of the trunks: these should

Aka-Ezo-Matsu (Saghalien Spruce), a young plant grown by cutting.

Sugi (Japanese Ceder) grown by wiring and nipping.

36

The so-called conifers, including the various species of pine, such as Ezo-Matsu (Saghalien Spruce), Shimpaku (Chinese Juniper), Sugi (Japanese Cedar), Toshō (Needle Juniper), are particularly well suited to the demands of bonsai, as many have dwarf varieties which easily lend themselves to growing as miniature plants.

What are some rules that bonsai growers must bear in mind?

●Put your young bonsai in a small container with good drainage, give it plenty of water, and place it in a semi-shaded spot outdoors.
●Once your plant has developed roots, place it on a shelf outside (bonsai should never be placed directly on the ground) where it will receive plenty of air and sunlight.
●It is essential to water your bonsai whenever the surface of the soil in the container becomes dry.
●Fertilize occasionally.
●New buds should be thinned just about the time the leaves take on a mature shape.
●Remove all insects and pests.
●In winter, proper protective measures must be taken to prevent the soil in the container from freezing.
●Transplant every one to two years. Bonsai grow in small containers, which are considered to be the smallest space in which a plant can survive. If left alone, the roots will fill up the container, absorbing all the nutrients in the soil and keeping new roots from developing, thus leading to the death of the bonsai. By transplanting the bonsai, you can check the condition of its roots. However, if the period for transplanting is missed, the roots will decay, the leaves will lose their natural color and may even die. In addition, the surface of the earth will become hard due to the overgrowth of the roots, so that any water given to the bonsai will eventually leak through and not be properly absorbed. Transplanting should be done in spring just before the new sprouts appear. (see illustrations p.31-32)

These are the basic rules which, if followed faithfully, will gradually turn your young plant into a genuine bonsai.

Don't bonsai require a lot of work?

While there is no end to the potential care that you may bestow on your bonsai, generally speaking they require less attention than ordinary potplants. This is especially true if one acquires the knack of tending bonsai—watering when the soil is dry, applying fertilizer before it is exhausted, nipping the buds when they have grown too big, etc. If you can get into the habit of performing these tasks regularly you will be able to avoid a lot of unnecessary work. Put simply, if you take the time to master the techniques, the art of bonsai growing requires only the minimum of effort.

It is important, however, to keep in mind that bonsai are plants that are growing not in the ground, but in small pots, so their care has certain rigid requirements. If there is no one to look after them continuously throughout the year, or if they can be looked after only on Sundays, success in this art could be extremely difficult!

How many years does it take to make a bonsai?

While the actual number of years required for a given plant to develop into a bonsai depends on a multitude of factors—the species used, the technique used to develop its form and arrange its branches, its environment, the amount of care given to the plant, the ability of the grower, etc.—the table opposite gives the average number of years required for some of the plants most commonly grown as bonsai.

How many years will my bonsai last?

The longevity of a bonsai depends on the species and the care it is given. However, with the exception of bamboo species, which are relatively short-lived (a mere 74 years at most!), there are few whose life span will not exceed 50 years. With the proper care given at the proper time, all other species last from 60 to 70 years, and some even several centuries. Pine species in particular, as well as such species as Ume (Flowering Japanese Apricot), Boke (Flowering Japanese Quince), Momiji (Japanese Maple), Tō-kaede (Trident Maple), Keyaki (Zelkova-tree), Buna (Japanese Beech), Karin (Chinese Quince), last so long that their lifespan is beyond speculation.

Years required	Species	Materials	Planting	Remarks
1–2 years	Kusa-Boke (Maule's Quince)	Young plant taken from the mountains	Several plants planted together	Only plants with branches and good blossoms should be used.
3 years	Miyama Kirishima-Tsutsuji (*Rhododendron kiusianum*)	From a 1–2 year-old grafted plant.	Single plant	Container should be 12 cm (5 inches). Buds should be nipped to keep the plant compact.
5–6 years	Tsubaki (Garden Camellia)	1 year-old seedling	Single plant	Main stem should be pruned to keep plant about 30cm/12 inch tall. Branches should be developed, and the plant made to blossom.
5–6 years	Yama-Gaki (Wild Japanese Persimmon)	1 year-old grafted plant	Single plant	Use a persimmon plant that has been grafted onto a 2 year-old persimmon seedling
5-6 years	Ume (Japanese Apricot)	4-5 year-old seedling	Single plant	First grow the plant in the garden and prune its branches each year.
5–6 years	Beni-Shitan (*Cotoneaster horizontalis*)	1 or 2 year liner from cutting	Single plant	Main stem should be pruned to keep the plant about 20 cm/8 inch tall. Branches should be developed, and the plant encouraged to bear berries.
7–8 years	Aka-Ezo-Matsu (Saghalien Spruce); Shimpaku (Chinese Juniper)	Plant propagated by grafting, or 3 year-old cutting	Single plant	Buds should be nipped frequently to shape branches.
7–8 years	Keyaki (Zelkova-tree) Soro; (Loose-flowered Hornbeam) Momiji (Maple); Kaede (Maple)	1 year-old seedling	Single plant or several planted together	
10 years	Kuro-Matsu (Japanese Black Pine); Goyō-Matsu (Five-Needled Pine)	Young plant	Single plant or several planted together	New buds should be nipped closely, and the branches should be arranged by wiring.
15 years and over	Aka-Matsu (Japanese Red Pine)	1 year-old seedling	Single plant	

70–80-year old Ume (Flowering Japanese Apricot)

GUIDE TO GROWING BONSAI

The first step for a beginner is to buy a cheap plant. A bonsai is quite different from an ordinary pot-plant, and it is advisable not to spend too much money until the important techniques of caring for one have been mastered.

Of course, by purchasing a fully developed bonsai you could enjoy viewing from day one, but such a plant will be expensive and can be difficult to maintain in its original condition.

If you wish to enjoy the art of bonsai it really is best to take a do-it-yourself approach: buy a cheap but healthy young tree and follow the method outlined in this book. If you follow these instructions meticulously, then after a couple of years you will have mastered the method of bonsai growing. From then on it will be up to you how far you choose to

Goyō-matsu (Five-Needled Pine) is hardy and easy to grow.

41

take your art. This is certainly best way to master the art of bonsai.

Species that are recommended for beginners

The following plants are suggested for beginners in the art of bonsai. Each species listed lends itself to growth as bonsai.

(1) Conifers or needle-leafed evergreens: Kuro-Matsu (Japanese Black Pine), Goyō-Matsu (Five-Needled Pine), Aka-Ezo-Matsu (Saghalien Spruce), Sugi (Japanese Cedar), Toshō (Needle Juniper), Shimpaku (Chinese Juniper); are especially valued for their leaves.

(2) Broad-leafed evergreens: Kuchinashi (Cape Gardenia), Tsubaki (Camellia), Sazanka (Sasanqua), Cha (Tea-plant) are prized for both their flowers and their general appearance.

(3) Small-leafed evergreens: Beni-Shitan (Rock Cotoneaster), Tachibana-modoki (Narrow-leaf Firethorn) are especially noted for their berries.

(4) Deciduous trees: Ume (Flowering Japanese Apricot), Boke (Flowering Japanese Quince), Sanzashi (Chinese Hawthorn), Kaidō (Showy Crab Apple), No-Bara (Japanese Dog Rose), Kirishima-Tsutsuji (Kirishima Azalea), Satsuki (Satsuki Azalea), Sarusuberi or Hyakujikko (Crape Myrtle) are much prized for their flowers. Momiji (Japanese Maple), Tō-kaede (Trident Maple), Keyaki (Zelkova), Buna (Japanese Beech), Soro (Loose-Flowered Hornbeam) and Tsuta (Japanese Ivy) are sought after for their leaves. Yusura-Ume (*Prunus tomentosa* Thunb.) is highly valued for its flowers and fruit. Gumi (Elaeagnus), Hime-Ringo (Nagasaki Crab Apple), Karin (Chinese Quince), Ume-modoki (*Ilex serrata* var. Sieboldii), and Kuko (Boxthorn) are particularly valued for their fruit.

Choosing a tree for practice

Listed above are several varieties which are easy to obtain and lend themselves to growing as bonsai. However, when choosing your tree, do keep the following factors in mind.

Suitable season
It is best to start when plants can be transported easily and when they can be transplanted without fear of damage. As a rough guide:
●Needle-leafed evergreens: October or November, or during spring budding.
●Evergreen broad-leafed trees: During spring budding or as young leaves are maturing.
●Small-leafed evergreens: During spring budding.
●Deciduous trees: In warmer districts, after the leaves have fallen; in colder districts, before spring budding.

Fire Thorn (left), Shimpaku (Chinese Juniper) (center), and Beni-Shitan (Rock Cotoneaster) (right), are all hardy and easy to grow.

Satsuki (Satsuki Azalea) is easy to grow and bears particularly beautiful flowers.

Momiji (Japanese Maple) is prized for its autumnal tints and also for the appearance of the tree in winter.

Choice of plant

Although there may be some difference between ordinary seedlings and plants that have been grown especially for bonsai, you should look for the same characteristics in whichever you decide to buy.

Select a plant which is not too tall, has a strong trunk which thickens near the roots, and has many visible roots. It must have small, dense leaves, and you must be sure that it is free from harmful insects and diseases.

Preferably, choose a tree with leaves that will be beautiful throughout the four seasons. If you want a plant which also has blossoms and fruit, avoid species with garish and colorful flowers and fruits as preference is traditionally given to species whose flowers or fruits provide an elegant and understated display.

You should choose a plant that already has an attractive arrangement of branches, although often, in the case of seedlings or trees grown by cutting or grafting, those without branches or those whose joints of grafting are too obvious are used for practice. In the case of branchless seedlings, it is best to choose a specimen which has healthy buds in the lower part of its trunk. In the case of seedlings or cuttings that have strong roots but have grown too tall, the top third of the plant should be cut off. At the same time, cut the main root off as short as possible. Other small roots can also be cut to fit the container. In the case of grafted trees, be careful to choose plants with perfect joints, as this will ensure the healthy growth of the tree, and to avoid those in which the grafting is obvious.

Container and soil preparation

Planting directly into a container

It is best to purchase a tree that has been growing in the ground for a year or two, as this will have given the roots and branches a good chance to develop. Once the plant has grown thick branches, a strong trunk and a good root system it can be transplanted into a container after the the roots and branches have been pruned.

Some plants, however, will have been grown from scratch in a container so that they could be cared for more easily. If a plant already has a reasonably good root system and abundant leaves, there is no harm in doing this. Still, even if you have only purchased a tree on which to practice your skills, it is always best to transplant it to check that it has been planted properly, that the soil is suitable and that the roots are healthy. Before transplanting, you will need to prepare your container and soil.

Karin (Chinese Quince) is prized for its hardiness and long life, as well as its beauty.

The container

An inexpensive unglazed or semi-hard baked pot with good water drainage and retention is recommended. Choose your pot carefully as its shape and size must be appropriate for your plant; you want to achieve a sense of balance between your tree and its pot. The container must have a hole at the bottom for good aeration and water drainage. Larger holes are better as they help to prevent root decay.

Wash your newly-purchased container thoroughly. If you have bought an old container, be sure to clean it thoroughly to eliminate the possibility of disease.

The container should be used only after all the water has completely drained.

The soil

The most suitable soil depends to some extent on your choice of plant and also varies from climate to climate. Generally, however, the most productive soil has the following characteristics:

- Good water retention and drainage, and good fertilizer absorption.
- Not too much fertilizer (if you know at the start that your soil is relatively free of fertilizer you will be able to add more as your plant requires it).
- No diseases and no eggs or larvae of injurious insects.
- Neither highly acidic nor highly alkaline.
- No poisonous substance injurious to plant growth.

Since soil from the average garden will rarely meet all these requirements, soil of this type must be prepared by mixing. Traditionally, five basic soil types are mixed to achieve the perfect soil. These five types are described below. Approximations of each type should be easy to find at most nurseries.

Types and characteristics of basic soils

The most widely used basic soils are as follows:

(a) Kurodama-tsuchi (Black loam).

Obtained from the lower strata of uplands, this is a soft, brownish-black, clayey loam. It contains little fertilizer, is clean, holds water well, absorbs fertilizer easily, and is slightly acidic.

This kind of soil contains hard lumps which will not break up, even after being mixed with other soils. Any soil with these characteristics may be used, but if it is too acidic the result will be the same as if too much fertilizer had been applied: the leaves will turn yellow and fall without bearing any flowers or fruit. This is the basic type of soil which should suit all bonsai.

(b) Akadama-tsuchi (Red Clay).

Red clay was once found in the highlands in and around Tokyo at a depth of 60 to 90 cm/24 to 36 inch. It is a heavy reddish-brown clay soil, and has similar properties to those of black loam. Its lumps are similarly hard to break up, so it both holds and drains water easily and is a good insu-

Containers for growing bonsai.

lator against heat and cold. It is also a good soil for promoting the growth of moss (in bonsai, the growth of moss on the soil surface in the container is considered an additional beauty.) Because of these characteristics, red clay is considered one of the essential basic clays. In Japan, the soil most commonly used is red soil, but other types, such as river or mountain sand, can be used with equally satisfactory results. Red clay is generally combined with sand. For pine and oak varieties, use in a 6:7 or 3:4 ratio. For other varieties, a ratio of 9:1 is used, and the sand may be replaced by fuyōdo (decomposed leaves).

(c) Coarse sand.

Coarse sand consists of broken fragments of rocks and stones. There are different varieties, such as mountain, river and sea sand. Of these, the kinds traditionally considered to be the best suited for use as a basic soil in Japan are sand from the Tenjin River, which is granitic, or Asama or Kiryu sand, both of which are volcanic.

(d) Kuro-poka.

This is also called Poka soil, and forms the surface layer of uplands in the hilly districts of Tokyo. It is a light, fine clayey loam and has a blackish color. It contains considerable amounts of fertilizer, holds water well and absorbs fertilizer easily. However, because its particles are small and easily breakable, it tends to have poor drainage, and should therefore be used sparingly. This soil is suitable for Keyaki, Momiji, Kaede, Zakuro and oak varieties.

(e) Grandma sop.

This soil is said to be the product of the weathering process on volcanic rocks, and is found in the stratum beneath the topsoil. It is very porous and consists of soft grains. When moist, it turns a beautiful yellowish-brown color; when dry, it is a pale yellowish-white color. It also becomes as light as ash when dry. This soil contains a very small amount of fertilizer and absorbs water and fertilizer well. Regardless of the amount of water it has absorbed, this soil will maintain its granular form for a long time thus retaining good air and water permeability. As water and air can flow through easily, the roots will not suffocate. It is quite acidic.

(f) Fuyōdo (Leaf Mold).

This soil is the product of dead leaves that have fallen onto the ground, decomposed and been absorbed into the soil. It is rich in organic nutri-

ents. Leaf mold keeps the temperature and humidity of the soil constant, thus making it soft and light, and allowing air and water to flow through easily. This ensures the healthy growth of the roots.

(g) Kanuma-tsuchi (Kanuma Soil).

This yellowish-brown soil is found in the Kanuma region of the Gunma Prefecture. It has good air and moisture-holding capacity. It is the preferred soil for grafted trees and is used as the bottom layer for cuttings. Also suitable for Tsutsuji and Satsuki trees.

Preparation of basic soil

When you are ready to put your soil into a container in preparation for planting your tree, it should be arranged with large grains at the bottom, medium grains in the middle, and small grains at the top. If you are starting with soil from the garden, rather than purchasing the above variety of soils, you will need to sieve the particles so that you can sort them and arrange them thus. If the grains are not properly sifted and arranged in this order, every time water or fertilizer is applied or rain falls, the fine grains will sink to the bottom of the container, gradually mak-

Various kinds of sifted soil. From right, large lumps, medium lumps and small lumps.

Sieves: One frame which can sift the soil into four different kinds according to size of the grains.

ing the soil impermeable to water and air. This in turn will eventually lead to root decay.

To sift your soil, you must first dry it out. This is done most simply by putting it out in the sun. If the soil is not dry, the sieves will become clogged and sifting cannot be done satisfactorily. You will need three grades of sieve: 1.5 mm (¹⁄₁₆ inch), 5 mm (¼ inch), and 12 mm (½ inch) meshes should be prepared. The soil should first be sifted through the sieve with the 1.5 mm (¹⁄₁₆ inch) mesh. These fine particles should be removed or they will pack the soil when it is watered, hampering its drainage. Then sift the soil through the 5 mm (¼ inch) sieve to separate the medium-fine grains of earth. Lastly, use the 12 mm (½ inch) sieve to remove medium grains of earth. The grains of earth which remain in the sieve are the largest. The soil which is traditionally known in Japan as Kuro-dama-tsuchi (Black round loam) or Aka-dama-tsuchi (Red round clay) is obtained in this manner.

After the basic soil has been sifted and the particles graded and separated, put the largest grains at the bottom of the container to facilitate water drainage. Next, put the medium grains in and plant your tree. This grade of soil promotes water drainage and is favorable to root growth. Lastly, place the soil consisting of the smallest grains at the top to give the container a pleasing appearance. This soil need not always be used. The proportions in which to mix the various kinds of soils depends on the type of tree in question. (See the section on Soil in the chart Bonsai and their Care.)

Put the rest of the sifted soil away in separate boxes, in a dry place, so that it will always be ready for use if needed.

Planting your tree

How to trim the roots and branches

Do not water your tree the day before you plan to transplant it into its container; if the soil is dry it will be easier to remove from the roots. The next day, loosen the soil in the container by giving it a couple of hard blows with your fist. Then turn the container upside down, and remove your plant, soil and all, by pushing your finger through the hole in the bottom.

Next, remove about ⅓ of the old soil. When doing this, take care not to injure the roots and do not remove the soil from the finer roots as they are easily damaged. As shown in the illustration, a bamboo chopstick is traditionally used for this purpose, but any fine implement will do. Then cut about ⅓ of the thick roots off with a pair of sharp shears. About ⅓ of the tips of the fine roots should also be cut off.

After the roots have been trimmed, take a good look at your tree. If your tree only has a few branches, no pruning should be done at all. However, if the branches of your tree are too close together, thin them out. If any branches have grown too long so as to be out of proportion, they too should be cut to improve the general appearance of the tree. If you remove a large branch, smooth over the cut area with a knife to ensure quicker healing.

For the remaining branches, only cut off the tips of those that are too long. Always cut at an angle, and choose a point after a small healthy branch or bud to make your cut.

As before, smooth the cut area with a knife. If you

How to prune the roots and branches of young tree

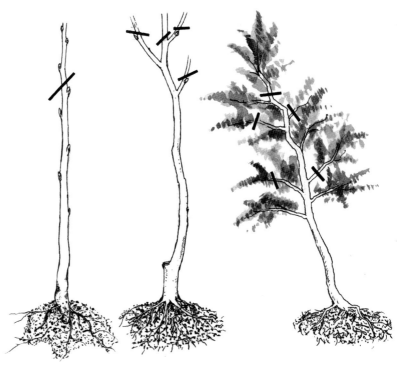

1 year-old seedling.   2 year-old grafted tree.   4 year-old plant grown from a cutting.

cut off a thick branch, consequently leaving a large wound, first smooth the area with a knife, then apply adhesive plaster or grafting wax. This prevents moisture from entering the exposed wood and stops it from drying out too much, either of which could cause decay.

Bud-nipping

Bud-nipping is the most important aspect of care that can be applied to a young bonsai. By cutting off the terminal buds you can prevent the branch from growing beyond the desired length, and encourage smaller side branches to sprout. Buds that are properly pruned will grow small, fine leaves in profusion, giving the bonsai an attractive, bushy appearance.

The manner of bud-nipping is govered by the variety of plant. In the case of Keyaki (Zellkova), buds will appear anywhere on the branch, but in the case of Goyō-Matsu (Five-Needled Pine), Kuro-Matsu (Japanese Black Pine), or Ezo-Matsu (Saghalian Spruce), buds will only grow from spicific sites. You will find details on bud-nipping techniques for specific species in sections V and VI.

Planting

Place your container on a worktable at a suitable height. If your worktable can also turn, so much the better. (See illustration.) Next, cover the hole at the bottom of the container with a fragment of clay pot or with fine plastic net (1.5 mm/½ inch mesh). This will stop the soil from dropping out of the container and prevents harmful insects from entering through the hole. Next, put in some large-grained soil to facilitate water drainage. Then, put in some

soil consisting of medium grains. You are now ready to plant your tree. Plant it right in the center of the container with its best side on view. Take care not to plant the tree too deep, as this will conceal the point where the roots spring from the base of the trunk, and this area is a feature of bonsai. Plant your tree so that this part is slightly above the edge of the container.

Next, add more medium-grained soil around the roots of the tree. This soil should be added slowly, in three or four layers. After adding each layer, gently press it down with a bamboo chopstick so that the soil fills the container evenly. This must be done very carefully, so as not to compact the soil and fill the spaces between the sifted grains. If these spaces are filled, the soil will become hard and will tend to retain water. Excessive water retention is particularly harmful to evergreens, many of which require very little water. Another reason to be gentle is that, in the case of plants that bear flowers, fruits or leaves, the

How to remove a plant from the container

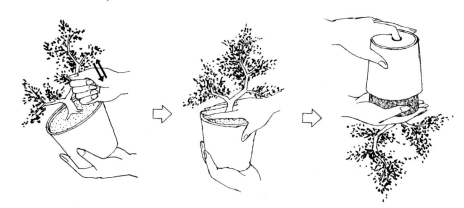

How to remove the old soil and cut the roots

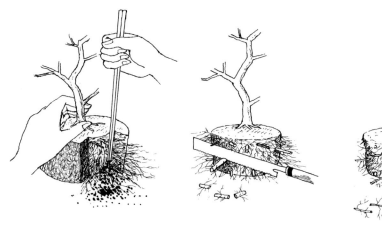

Remove 1/3 of the old soil.   Cut all thick roots with a saw.   Prune medium sized roots with a pair of shears.

48

roots are fine and could be damaged. After this your container should be about ¾ full.

After the tree has been planted, place the fine-grained soil on the top to improve the general appearance. These grains can then be pressed down gently with a flat trowel or a piece of wood.

You should now water your plant. This should be done from above, using a watering can with a fine rose, so that the entire tree is moistened. Stop water-ing as soon as water starts running out of the hole at the bottom of the container.

Where to keep your bonsai

For the first week or two, put your newly-planted bonsai in a spot that is sheltered from the wind, to allow the plant to take root properly, but where it will catch two to three hours of morning sun.

Steps and technique for planting a tree

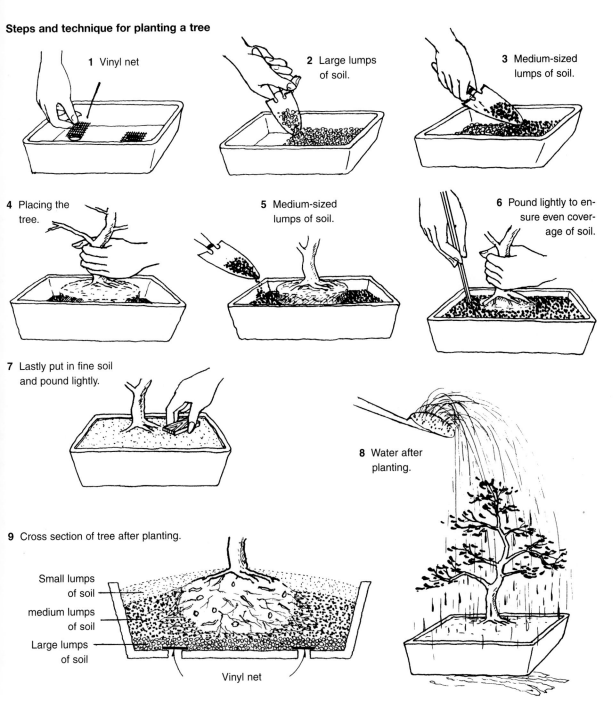

1 Vinyl net

2 Large lumps of soil.

3 Medium-sized lumps of soil.

4 Placing the tree.

5 Medium-sized lumps of soil.

6 Pound lightly to ensure even coverage of soil.

7 Lastly put in fine soil and pound lightly.

8 Water after planting.

9 Cross section of tree after planting.

Small lumps of soil

medium lumps of soil

Large lumps of soil

Vinyl net

During this period the plant should not be exposed to the cold or to heavy rain. It should be watered regularly to prevent the soil from drying, and should not be brought inside.

After this, the plant should be exposed to plenty of sunlight and air, preferably on a strong shelf built outdoors. Deciduous trees need special attention as in summer their leaves may be damaged by strong direct sunlight, and in winter their branches may be damaged by frost. In particular, Ume-modoki (*Ilex serrata* var. Sieboldii), Momiji (Japanese Maple) and Tō-Kaede (Trident Maple) require protection against frost, although such protection against the cold should only be just sufficient to keep the soil in the container from freezing. It is not suitable to protect your plant by placing it in the ground, pot and all. Unlike potted flowering plants, if a potted bonsai is placed in the ground the moss at the base of the trunk and the bark will be damaged.

Watering and fertilizer application

Watering
Ideally, clean rain water or city water should be kept in a tank built near the shelf for bonsai to keep it at

Showing how bonsai should placed. (Author's garden)

practically the same temperature as that of the atmosphere. This is because the sudden change in temperature caused by the application of cold water can damage the leaves of a plant. However, there is no danger of such damage if the plant is accustomed to cold water from the time it starts budding in spring.

You will need a watering-can with two roses, one with large holes and the other with fine. The roses should be changed to suit the occasion.

Three methods of watering are used. The first is to water only around the roots, and the second to apply water so as to moisten the trunk, the branches and both sides of the leaves. The latter method is called syringing. The former method should be used whenever the surface of the soil in the container becomes whitish and dry. A rose with small holes should be used when syringing or after transplanting while the soil has not yet settled. Otherwise, use a rose with large holes. The third method is called

Keep a tank of water near the bonsai so that it will be at the same temperature as your bonsai.

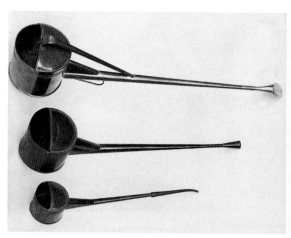

Watering cans.

springing, and refers to moistening the leaves. This should be done after transplanting, before the roots develop, and in summer when it is hot and dry. It is only through experience that you will learn how and when your tree needs watering, as varying situations and climates will make a difference. For instance, when the edge of the container is much higher than the soil surface, water will tend to accumulate in the container as a result of excessive watering. If, however, the container's edge is too low, water will overflow and may leave the plant too dry. Plants with mature root systems will absorb water more readily. Some species, such as Ume (Flowering Japanese Apricot), Momiji (Japanese Maple) and Tō-kaede (Trident Maple) generally require a lot of water, but the amount of water needed will vary with the type of tree, the soil, and the manner of planting.

A general rule to follow is to water once or twice a day in spring and autumn, from two to three times a day in summer, and once every fourth or fifth day in winter. In fine weather, newly transplanted trees should be watered once a day. In summer, plants with mature root systems may need watering once a day, early in the morning or in the evening, or twice a day, once in the morning and once in the evening.

In summary, just remember that water is absolutely essential to all plants, but is even more so in the case of bonsai as they are planted in small containers with a limited amount of soil and an equally limited capacity for the retention of water. They have no other source of water except rain, dew, and artificial watering. Thus, the absolute importance of watering should be fully recognized and practiced in bonsai growing. But take care, as overwatering can have a negative effect on the growth of branches and leaves, resulting in poor flowers and fruits. Under such circumstances, the tree will be susceptible to attack by diseases and insects and, in extreme cases, the roots can suffocate and cause the plant's death. Hence watering should be done in response to both the dryness of the soil in the container and the color and growth of the leaves. In short, the fundamental principle in watering is neither too much nor too little.

Fertilizer

Fertilizer is to plants what food is to human beings. In the case of bonsai, you have a plant living in a very limited amount of soil, which can only contain the minimum amount of fertilizer, and yet you want it to develop a thick trunk, branches and leaves. Bonsai must also bear the stress of having all unwanted branches pruned and, depending on the kind of tree,

must be made to bear flowers and fruits. The need for fertilizer is only too obvious. Without proper fertilizer application, proper plant growth cannot be expected. But too much fertilizer will be as harmful as too little and will injure the roots of the plant. The best fertilizer for bonsai, especially for bonsai which is in the process of growing, should contain three elements: nitrogen, phosphate and potassium in the proportion of $5:3:2$. Nitrogen helps the growth of roots, branches and leaves. If an insufficient amount is applied, leaves will turn a yellowish-brown. Phosphate also ensures the healthy growth of roots, branches and leaves, as well as flowers and fruit, but take care not to use too much of it in oak or pine species. Finally, potassium is necessary to ensure the healthy growth of the tree as a whole. If it is not applied in sufficient amounts, the leaves will turn a yellowish-brown; in addition, both the leaves and fruit will decay and fall. You can use organic fertilizer, chemical fertilizer or a combination of both. There are liquid as well as solid fertilizers. Solid organic fertilizer is considered the best. Oil cake, bone meal and rice bran are the most balanced of fertilizers. Traditionally, rapeseed cake is the ideal fertilizer for bonsai. If you can get hold of it, its use is described below. If not, a fertilizer, or a combination of fertilizers, which contain the above elements in the prescribed proportions should be available at your nursery.

Three methods of rapeseed cake fertilizer application

(1) Application in liquid form. Dilute 1.8 liters of rapeseed cake with three times that amount of water, and allow the mixture to decompose thoroughly. After the rapeseed cake has formed a sediment, the liquid at the top should be diluted with another 5 to 15 times the same amount of water. This should be applied to the roots, but not to the base of the trunk itself. The liquid diluted with five times the same amount of water is considered strong, and that diluted with fifteen times the same amount of water is considered weak. The weak liquid fertilizer should be used from spring to summer, and the strong from summer to autumn.

This liquid obtained from rapeseed cake is ready for use after three weeks in midsummer, and after two months in winter.

(2) Application in powdered form. Two or three lumps of powdered rapeseed cake may be put on the surface of the container soil. The amount of powder in each lump should not exceed 1 to 2 small tea-

Three ways of giving fertilizer

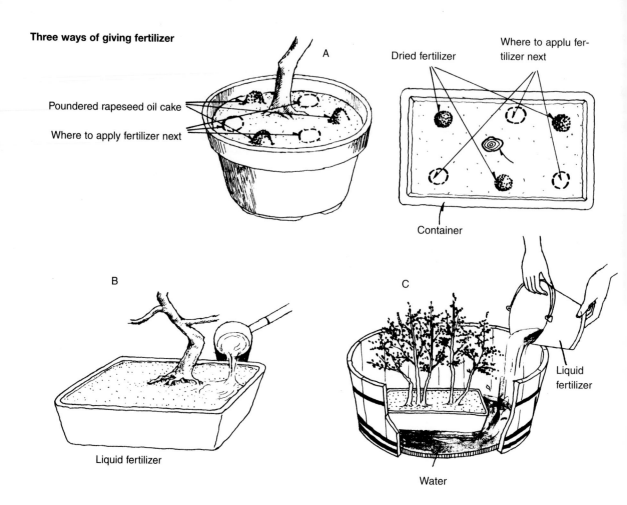

A

Poundered rapeseed oil cake

Where to apply fertilizer next

Dried fertilizer

Where to applu fertilizer next

Container

B

C

Liquid fertilizer

Liquid fertilizer

Water

spoonsful. The powder will gradually ferment and decompose and, in about three to four weeks, will begin to take effect as fertilizer. The lumps should be placed in different places the second time. This method is called depositing fertilizer.

(3) Application in dried form. Rapeseed cake can also be kneaded with water, and made into round balls about two or three centimetres in diameter. Place the balls in a shaded airy place to let them ferment, dry and harden. The method of application is then similar to that used for powdered fertilizer. Place two or three balls separately on the surface of the soil. As the fertilizer is already fermented, the balls will start acting as fertilizer in about two weeks.

The above methods describe how to use rapeseed cake. If you do use rapeseed cake you will need additional fertilizer to provide phosphate and potassium. A good blood and bone fertilizer can be used to provide the phosphate, and potash will provide potassium.

Application period

Whatever method you use, the time to add fertilizer is from when buds appear in early spring to about mid-July, and from the end of August to the early part of September. But even during these periods do not fertilize immediately after transplanting or, in the case of fruit-bearing trees, before the fruits have fully ripened or while they are flowering. It's also better to skip fertilizing in rainy weather and on hot summer days. In the case of weak liquid fertilizer (consisting of the decomposed liquid of rapeseed cake diluted with 15 times the same amount of water), application once a week is plenty; in the case of strong liquid fertilizer, apply once every two weeks, and for powdered and dried fertilizers, apply once a month. It is possible to use liquid, powdered and dried fertilizer in combination, but make sure you change the number of applications appropriately.

Apart from the points listed above, keep in mind the following when applying fertilizer:

(a) Adjust the number of applications in response to the growth of the buds, the color of the leaves, and the general health of the tree.

(b) Do not apply fertilizer when the soil in the container is dry. In this case, water the soil before applying fertilizer. If you apply fertilizer to dry soil, the result is the same as if strong fertilizer had been applied.

(c) There is no point in applying fertilizer on rainy days, as it will just be washed away and wasted.

(d) As early summer is the time when young leaves reach maturation, this is when the tree has the greatest need for fertilizer and applications should be increased accordingly. Applications in midsummer, when temperatures are high, only injure the roots. Do not apply fertilizer again until autumn when the tree is ready to enter its dormant period during the winter.

(e) If the primary feature of your tree is its fruit, make sure you give it plenty of phosphate and a little more than the ordinary amount of potassium when it begins to bear fruit.

How to nip the buds

If a tree planted in a container is taken care of as described on page 49, it will develop both strong roots and new buds. To stimulate the new growth, keep your plant well watered and fertilized, and put it on an outdoor shelf where it will get plenty of sun. This will also stimulate the sprouting of new buds on the trunk and branches and, sometimes, in the case of grafted trees, new buds will appear on the stock.

Why pruning is necessary

If all the new buds are allowed to grow, the shape of the tree will become uneven. Buds that are well placed will grow strongly, while others that are crowded or in the shade may become stunted and look unattractive. To avoid this, as soon as the new buds begin to grow, some will need to be removed. This is called bud-nipping.

The purpose of bud-nipping

Besides the above, there are other reasons why bud-nipping is necessary.

(a) It prevents new shoots from getting out of hand and growing longer than is desirable, and helps the growth of underdeveloped buds. In plants grown for their flowers or fruits, bud-nipping promotes the healthy development of flower buds.

(b) It helps the tree to grow an extensive and attractive branch structure. In the case of autumn Momiji (Japanese Maple) and other winter trees, which are grown primarily to enjoy the appearance of the tree after the leaves have fallen, it is essential that the ends of the branches are encouraged to be fine, soft and dense.

(c) It reduces the useless consumption of nutrition, and allows more sunlight and better air circulation to the tree.

(d) It improves the appearance of the tree, the development of the branches and leaves, and also the condition of the fruit by controlling the growth of the trunk and thick branches which constitute the main outline of the tree.

When and how to nip the buds

Both the timing and manner of bud-nipping vary with the kind of tree. Some varieties require bud-nipping only once, while others require it several times.

(a) Kuro-Matsu (Japanese Black Pine), Goyō-Matsu (Five-Needled Pine). Nip the buds when the new buds have come out and are still soft but before the leaves have developed. The longer buds should be nipped with a pair of shears, so as to leave a little portion of the base. If four or five buds have sprouted from one spot, cut off one or two from the base, then nip the buds which have been left. Bud-nipping needs to be done only once.

(b) Aka-Ezo-Matsu (Saghalien Spruce). When the egg-shaped buds (see illustration) begin to open their leaves, bud-nipping should be done once with one's fingernails. However, as the buds are numerous, it will be necessary to do this every day during the budding season.

(c) Sugi (Japanese Cedar), Toshō (Needle Juniper). Whenever the buds begin to open their leaves, nip the tips of the unwanted buds using your fingernails. However, at places where you want a new branch to grow, leave the bud un-nipped.

(d) Shimpaku (Chinese Juniper). The buds at the center of the tips should be nipped whenever new buds appear.

(e) Ume (Flowering Japanese Apricot), Boke (Flowering Japanese Quince), Kaidō (Showy Crab Apple), Sanzashi (Chinese Hawthorn), Sakura (Flowering Cherry), Tsubaki (Camellia), Hime-Ringo (Nagasaki Crab Apple), Karin (Chinese Quince), Ume-modoki (*Ilex Serrata* var. Sieboldii). Unwanted buds should be nipped from the base as soon as they appear, while the remaining buds should be allowed to

How to nip shoots

Shimpaku

Satsuki

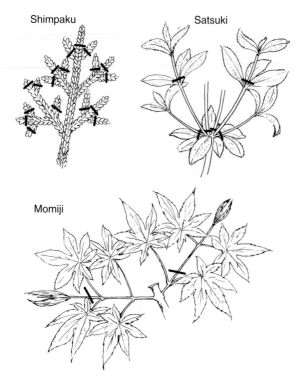

Ume

Aka-Ezo-Matsu

Kuro-Matsu

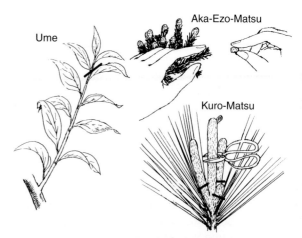

Momiji

grow. When the new leaves have all come out, the ends of those branches which have grown too long should be nipped once.

However, in the case of Ume-modoki (*Ilex Serrata* var. Sieboldii), which bears fruits on the young branches that have come out in the same year, it is best to leave a good number of flowers or fruits at bud-nipping time.

(f) Satsuki (Satsuki Azalea). As several shoots will emerge from the same bud, wait until all the shoots have appeared, then keep one or two that seem to be growing well and are positioned where you want a new branch to grow, and clip off the rest at the base. Nip the remaining shoots, leaving two or three leaves. Follow the same procedure for all the branches. Buds that are crowded together should also be nipped.

(g) Roses. Follow the same procedure as for Ume (Flowering Japanese Apricot), but do not nip too deep. Nipping should be limited to the main buds at the end.

(h) Momiji (Japanese Maple), Tō-kaede (Trident Maple), Soro (Loose Flower Hornbeam), Nire-Keyaki (Chinese Elm). It is essential that these trees are grown so that the ends of the branches are fine, soft and dense. To achieve this, nip new buds repeatedly from after budding-time in

Keyaki (Zelkova) whose shoots have been nipped several times to make the tips of the branches fine, soft and dense.

spring until the leaves change color in autumn.

(i) Kaki (Japanese Persimmon), Kuri (Japanese Chestnut). It is better not to prune the buds until the tree has borne fruit, provided that this does not cause the tree to lose its symmetry.

Some important points to bear in mind when bud-nipping

(a) A tree that has been transplanted and had its roots or branches trimmed should not have any buds nipped until it has fully recovered.

(b) The timing of nipping for trees that require bud-nipping only once is very important. If it is done too late, the appearance of secondary buds

54

may be delayed and, as a result, these may be damaged by cold in winter. But if it is done too early you may ruin the future appearance of the branches.

(c) Plants such as Boke (Japanese Quince), Satsuki (Satsuki Azalea) and roses tend to sprout a profusion of buds from the trunk, branches, and even from the stock on which grafting has been done. For these plants it is important to remove, from the base, all buds that look weak, as soon as they appear, as these tend to grow into long, weak branches. If this pruning is done after the bud has grown large, unattractive scars will be left, detracting from the overall appearance of your bonsai.

(d) If a tree is pruned too frequently, it will suffer and become unhealthy. You should therefore always pay attention to the general health of your plant and ensure that bud-nipping is carried out in the right way and at the right time.

(e) Soft new buds may be nipped with the fingernails, but those which have hardened should be removed with shears.

Control of insects and disease

Both bonsai in containers and trees planted in the ground are subject to attacks from insects and disease which can affect the growth of the tree and mar its appearance. In extreme cases, such attacks can cause leaves or fruit to fall prematurely, leaves to wither, and even the death of the tree. Both disease and insect infestations can spread from one tree to another, but insects are particularly likely to do so.

Although insects and disease pose a genuine threat to bonsai, their control is often considered a tiresome and tedious task by beginners, and is thus neglected. Often no action is taken until the tree begins to wither, by which time it is too late.

It must therefore be stressed that careful watch should be kept for signs of disease or insect infestation and, if discovered, control measures should be carried out immediately.

Diseases of bonsai

(a) Root-Decay. This is the most damaging disease to which bonsai can fall victim, and there is hardly a variety of bonsai that is not susceptible to it. There are various causes. Failure to mix the soil in the proper proportions can lead to poor water drainage and a subsequent accumulation of water; the soil in the container may be too dry; transplanting may have been done at the wrong time; or too much water may have been applied after transplanting.

When a tree is attacked by this disease, its root system begins to decay, causing the leaves and branches to wither. This disease will ultimately lead to the death of the plant.

(b) Nematode worms. These cause wart-like swellings to develop at the base of the trunk or on the roots. The tree loses its vitality and eventually dies. Boke (Flowering Japanese Quince), Fuji (Japanese Wisteria) and Sakura (Flowering Cherry) are subject to it. In order to prevent the disease from spreading further and killing the plant, it is best to repot the bonsai immediately into clean and disease-free soil. During the process of changing the soil, the infectious bugs can be found and killed on the spot.

(c) Mildew. This makes the leaves and young branches of trees look as though they had been

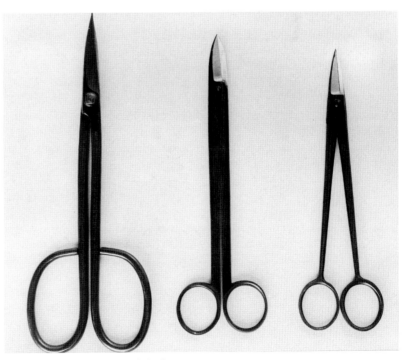

Kinds of shears used for bud-nipping.

sprayed with flour. It is common, especially in spring and autumn. Momiji (Japanese Maple), Tō-Kaede (Trident Maple), roses, Kaki (Japanese Persimmon), Hime-Ringo (Nagasaki Crab Apple), Karin (Chinese Quince), and Ume-modoki, (*Ilex serrata* var. Sieboldii) are particularly susceptible to it.

(d) Leaf spot. This causes large numbers of black, brown, or grey spots to appear on the leaves. Spots may also appear on young twigs, branches, and even on fruit. It most frequently affects deciduous trees, especially trees that are grown for their display of fruit.

(e) Rust. In this disease, lumps of rust-like powder of yellow, orange, brown, reddish-brown, grey or white appear on leaves and young shoots. It is very common in early summer. Sugi (Japanese Cedar), Tsutsuji (Azalea), Satsuki (Satsuki Azalea), roses, Yusura-Ume (*Prunus tomentosa* Thunb.), and Ume-modoki (*Ilex serrata* var. Sieboldii) are subject to this disease.

(f) Sooty mold. This is caused by parasites such as scales or aphids. The leaves and branches of affected plants look as if they had been sprayed with soot, and the tree appears unhealthy. This disease most frequently attacks plants that are positioned poorly and are not getting enough sunlight or air. Broad-leafed evergreens are subject to this disease.

Insects that attack bonsai

Insects that damage bonsai in other countries will differ from those found in Japan. However, in general, the following insects are the common enemies of bonsai:

(a) Insects that attack new shoots. The aphid is an insect that attacks the new shoots of all kinds of trees and sucks their sap. The web-worm and the ume bud moth attack all varieties of pine, Sugi (Japanese Cedar), Ume (Flowering Japanese Apricot), Sakura (Flowering Cherry), roses and apples. These insects eat their way into new buds. Stem borers eat their way into new shoots of pines.

(b) Insects that attack the leaves. Caterpillars and sawfly attack all varieties of pine. The Japanese cedar tussock moth eats the leaves of Sugi (Japanese Cedar) and Toshō (Needle Juniper). The looper or canker-worm eats the leaves of Ume (Flowering Japanese Apricot), Boke (Japanese Quince), roses, and Satsuki (Satsuki Azalea). Other injurious insects include pests

Control of the diseases stated above

Name of Disease	Means of Prevention	Means of Disease Control
Root-decay	Avoid the conditions listed above which will encourage disease.	Replant as soon as posssible. When replanting, cut off decayed roots and disinfect with mercury compounds.
Nematodes	When initially buying a tree, take care to choose one that is free from disease.	When transplanting, cut off the wart-like swellings, immerse in lime for about 10 minutes, then plant.
Mildew	Ensure that the plant gets sufficient sunlight and air. All fallen leaves should be burnt.	New soil should be used for each transplanting. Find a suitable preparation of an organic sulfur compound and spray it 2 or 3 times in the early stages of the disease.
Leaf spot	Burn any fallen leaves and fruit, and remove and burn withered branches.	Spray with solutions of dissolvable or liquid preparations of Bordeaux mixture.
Rust	Burn any fallen leaves.	Find a suitable insecticide and spray for two to three days in the early stages of the disease.
Sooty mold	Exterminate all scales and aphids.	Spray with machine oil in winter. Do not spray when the leaves are growing as it soils the leaves leaves and branches, and can harm the tree.

such as caterpillars, leaf rollers and bag worms.

(c) Insects that suck the sap from the leaves of trees. When infestation occurs, these pests can be found sticking to the backs of the leaves. Red spiders will attack most species, and tend to inflict damage in hot, dry weather. The lace bug attacks Kuro-Matsu (Japanese Black Pine), Ezo-Matsu (Saghalien Spruce), Satsuki (Satsuki Azalea) and Tsubaki (Camellia).

(d) Insects that attack buds and flowers. Sawflies and chafers.

(e) Insects that attack branches and trunks. The two most common are scale and ruby scale. Apart from these, wooly aphids most commonly infect deciduous trees. Borers dig tunnels into the wood of trunks and large branches, causing them to snap or wither.

(f) Insects that attack the roots. Cutworms eat the roots of trees.

Ants build nests in the roots of trees and injure their growth. Earthworms cause water leakage.

Control of the above insects

The important thing is to find a suitable insecticide and use it effectively to prevent the spread of insects as quickly as possible. But take care to use any insecticide sparingly, as your bonsai will have less protection against any side effects of the insecticide than a tree planted in the ground. Care must also be taken to avoid insecticides that will leave a residue on the plant and spoil its appearance.

Protecting your bonsai from the winter cold

(1) Hardy bonsai which can withstand the cold, such as Kuro-Matsu (Japanese Black Pine), Goyō-Matsu (Five-Needled Pine), Toshō (Needle Juniper) and Shimpaku (Chinese Juniper), may be left on an outdoor shelf throughout the winter. When a bonsai is left outdoors, however, the container should be tied firmly to the shelf by string or wire to prevent it from being blown over by the wind.

(2) Plants that need protection against cold. Even hardy plants which can withstand the cold should be protected against the cold if they have been transplanted recently and have not yet developed roots, or if there is any danger of having their branches broken under the weight of snow.

All plants that may be susceptible to cold should be placed where they will not be exposed to direct sunlight and be well protected against the cold. This includes natives of warm climates which will have little resistance to cold, plants like Keyaki (Zelkova), Momiji (Japanese Maple) and Tō-Kaede (Trident Maple) whose branches wither easily in winter, and those that blossom early in spring, such as Ume (Flowering Japanese Apricot) and Boke (Japanese Quince).

Ways to protect your bonsai against the cold

(a) The simplest option is to put them under the eaves, near a window, or in a veranda, where they will be protected from wind, rain, frost, snow, and the harshest temperatures.

(b) Put the bonsai in a veranda, hallway, entrance, or sunroom where there will be plenty of light.

(c) Put the bonsai beneath a covered frame or in an unheated greenhouse.

(d) Bury the pot in the ground in a spot with good drainage and plenty of sunlight. Build a simple structure over the bonsai to protect it against frost.

(e) Make a waterproof cloth shelter for your bonsai that closes off the north, east and west-facing sides and the top. Leave the south side open to let in sunlight. On very cold days, close the south side too with a translucent paper or plastic film.

(f) Build a shelter with waterproof cloth or jute sacks around your bonsai shelf. On fine days, open the south side to let in air and sunlight.

(g) Dig a trench 60–100 cm (24–40 inches) deep in a spot where the drainage is good. Build a sloping roof or a three-quarter roof that stands about 30–90 cm (12–36 inches) high over the trench. The roof should slope toward the south. The other three sides, north, east and west, should be closed off with boards. On the south side there should be windows of frosted glass to let in sunlight. Place your bonsai on shelves inside the shelter. Steps may be made either on the east or west side to use as an entrance and exit. (See the illustration of cold-proof shelters in winter.)

When to protect your bonsai against the cold

Most bonsai should be placed in a cold-proof shelter after the frost season has set in and the plant has been exposed once or twice to light frost. However, plants which are easily damaged by frost should be placed in the shelter before the frost season begins. In spring, as soon as the temperature is warmer, bonsai should be returned to their outdoor shelf. This is done so that the first buds appear while they are outdoors and not indoors. If the buds first appear while they are outdoors, they will develop and harden more quickly, making them tougher and more resistant to any possible harm.

Care of bonsai in a cold-proof shelter

(a) Place tall trees on the north side of the shelter and smaller trees on the south, so as to provide maximum sunlight to all plants. Species that require a lot of light, such as Kuro-Matsu (Japanese Black Pine), Goyō-Matsu (Five-Needled Pine), Ezo-Matsu (Saghalien Spruce), Toshō (Needle Juniper), Shimpaku (Chinese Juniper), Ume (Flowering Japanese Apricot), Boke (Flowering Japanese Quince), Kaidō (Showy Crab Apple), Sakura (Flowering Cherry), and Keyaki (Zelkova), should be placed where plenty of light is available, while plants which do not require so much light in winter, such as Sugi (Japanese Cedar), Tō-Kaede (Trident Maple), Momiji (Japanese Maple), ivy, Ume-modoki (*Ilex serrata* var. Sieboldii), Sanzashi (Chinese Hawthorn), Hime-Ringo (Nagasaki Crab Apple), and Satsuki (Satsuki Azalea), should be placed where there is less light.

Examples of coldproof installation for winter.

Plants that have recently been transplanted and thus have not developed root systems, or plants whose trunks or branches have recently been cut to arrange the shape of the tree, should be placed at the farthest end in semi-shade.

(b) It is not necessary to put an actual heat source in the shelter, as its purpose is only to provide enough protection to prevent the soil in the container from freezing. Bonsai should not be brought into a heated room. If it must be put in such a room, it must be only for a short period of time, say a week or so, and you will need to be very careful to keep it well watered and not to let the soil dry out. A bonsai kept for too long in a heated room is likely to respond to the warmth by budding. If this occurs in winter, when the plant should be dormant, the plant will be weak when the time for proper activity comes.

(c) As at all times, water your bonsai whenever the surface of the soil in the container becomes white and dry. You will know when you have given your plant enough water when it begins to flow out of the hole at the bottom of the container. To replace the effect of dew, water should occasionally be syringed onto the leaves of the plant. As this method of watering is particularly good for Kuro-Matsu (Japanese Black Pine), Goyō-Matsu (Five-Needled Pine); Ezo-Matsu (Saghalien Spruce), Shimpaku (Chinese Juniper), Toshō (Needle Juniper), Ume (Flowering Japanese Apricot), Boke (Flowering Japanese Quince), Keyaki (Zelkova Tree), this should be done every other day or so.

(c) It is important to remember to air the shelter. Even in winter, the temperature can rise quite high during the daytime, and the shelter can become very humid as a result of evaporation. This excessive moisture is harmful to the plants. Therefore, during the daytime, the cover of the shelter should be removed to let in fresh air.

(e) As most trees are dormant during winter, no fertilizer is needed. But even in winter harmful insects are still a danger. You will therefore need to disinfect once or twice against such insects even though the tree is dormant.

(f) Turn the container that your bonsai is in occasionally so that every part of the tree gets enough light. This will ensure even budding in spring, and is a precaution that should be observed as much for plants placed outdoors as for those in a shelter.

(g) If in spring you suddenly remove the plant from

the cold-proof shelter and place it outdoors, the abrupt change in temperature could be harmful. To avoid this, remove the heavy covering for protecting the plant against frost several days before taking the plant out. This will accustom your plant to the outside air. Plants which bud first should be removed first.

If you care for your bonsai properly during its period of winter dormancy, it will develop into a fine tree in less than a year. Trimming the branches and improving the general appearance of the tree is the next step; but your efforts so far will have given you some idea of the pleasure of growing bonsai and will stimulate you to further efforts in future!

Example of a shelter for bonsai in winter.

BONSAI TOOLS

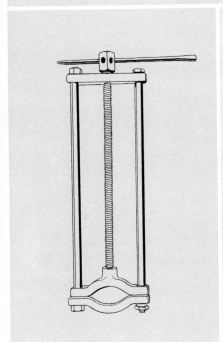

Jack, Kyuka type

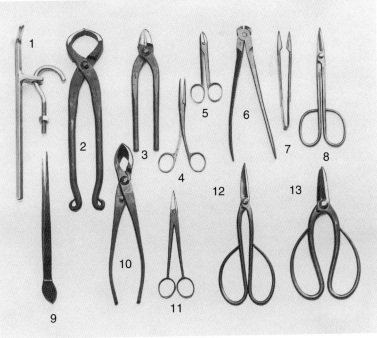

1. Lever, Kyuka type 2. Root cutter 3. Wire plieres, large 4. Wire remover 5. Wire cutter, nail-clipper for cutting fine wire 6. Wire cutter 7. Shears for leaf-cutting 8. Shears for pinching the shoots 9. Tweezers 10. Nipper for twig cutting 11. Bud nipping shears for pines and junipers 12. Trimming shears with long handle 13. Trimming shears

59

INTRODUCTION TO BRANCH ARRANGEMENT

Why arrange the branches?

Bonsai is an art that reveres nature. The fact is, however, that as bonsai grow in small containers with a limited amount of soil, they cannot be expected to grow long, thick branches and luxuriant foliage with the same vigour as trees that grow in the mountains and forests.

If a tree is grown for several years in a container its development will be hampered and as a result the tree will become compact. But the merely being small is not what makes a bonsai. As explained in the opening paragraph of this book, bonsai aspires to reproduce, in miniature, the appearance of ahuge old tree or a fragment of natural landscape.

To grow bonsai you will need to master certain special techniques other than those already mentioned. These consist chiefly of learning how to arrangethe trunk and branches, and are skills which no bonsai grower can afford to be without.

The aim of branch-arranging

Branch-arranging is done to correct and improve the shape of a plant by removing unnecessary branches. It also aims to straighten unsightly bends or to group or separate branches, taking care to enhance the natural characteristics of the tree. At the same time, branch-arranging aims to give the tree a sense of grace which will enhance the essential character of the tree and increase its value as a bonsai. Excessive bending or twisting of branches should be avoided.

Proficiency and knowledge are needed for branch arranging

Arranging the branches of a bonsai is no easy task. In fact, it is one of the most difficult techniques involved in the art of bonsai growing. For the task to be performed well, you must be able to visualize the ultimate shape of the tree and be equipped with the knowledge that will allow you toreach that goal without hurting the tree.

This may sound baffling to a beginner, but with the aid of this book, and by studying the methods used by more experienced bonsai artists, you can start with the easier methods and gradually master the whole art. The important thing is to be patient and to make a genuine effort to acquire the knowledge and the necessary skills, as the rewards will be many.

Once you have mastered the technique of branch-arranging you will be able to apply your knowledge to any bonsai of any species. And as your abilities improve you will find that your interest, too, increases proportionately.

Various ways to arrange branches

Generally speaking, the following three methods are used in branch-arranging. Each of these methods stems from the desire to capture, in bonsai, the appearance of large, old trees and the graceful shape of the trees depicted in Chinese paintings.

Arranging branches with a pair of shears

In this method, branches are arranged by cutting off unwanted buds and branches with shears. Two kinds of shears are needed, one for pruning branches and the other for nipping buds. However, it is not possible to perform such major operations as bending or straightening thick branches using shears alone. This technique is useful only in the basic stages of branch-arranging, since using shears for major surgery on the tree can create unsightly scars and leave the tips of the branches ragged.

Suspending the branches

This method consists of arranging branches by pulling them sideways or obliquely downwards with strong but soft twine or wire. Sometimes a piece of wood is also applied, like a splint, to the branch.

This technique can work well with trees that are soft and easily breakable, or with trees that have soft, easily scarred bark, such as Sugi (Japanese Cedar), Momiji (Japanese Maple), Tō-Kaede (Trident Maple), Keyaki (Zelkova), and Ume-modoki (*Ilex serrata* var. Sieboldii). It also tends to be the method used by people who have no confidence in arranging branches by wiring them. However, this is by no means the best or the safest method in all cases.

The two preceding methods were commonly used until about 1890, after which the art of bonsai growing was revolutionised by the discovery of how to arrange branches by wiring. This new method superceded the two older methods to the extent that neither is used much these days.

Arranging by wiring

This method consists of twisting wire around the trunk or branches of a tree, then bending or straightening them in the desired direction or angle. This is the most advanced and effective way to arrange branches. Its only drawback is that, to be done properly, it requires knowledge, skill and the proper tools. However, once the technique has been mastered, it can be used for a lifetime. Therefore, the method of arranging by wiring will be explained in

Example of arranging by pruning with shears

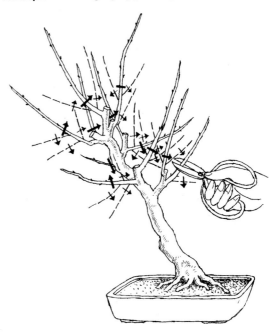

The arrow shows where the cut is to be made.
The dotted line shows where the young twigs will next appear.

Example of arranging by suspending the branches

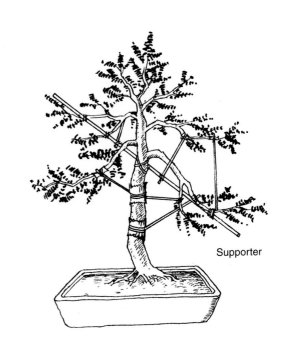

Supporter

61

this book because it is the method most commonly used at present.

Tools and materials needed for arranging by wiring

Tools:
The following tools are needed for branch-arranging by wiring: a pair of shears for cutting wood; another pair for making deep cuts; a small saw; a knife; a pair of pincers; a pair of pliers; a lever for arranging the branches; a revolving table. A jack, which is used to bend thick trunks or branches, may be necessary to make an acute bend in the trunk or in the thick branch of a tree that is particularly rigid. The jack was invented by the author and is available in Kyuka-en Garden, (see illustration p. 59). Any other similar tool may be used to the same effect. A lever is used to arrange branches that cannot be safely handled by hand. Other more common household tools may be required but they will be mentioned as we come to them.

Materials:
Wire
This is most important. There are many varieties of wire, including steel, iron, and zinc-coated iron, but none of these is suitable, as they are all too hard and difficult to handle. Moreover, they tend to rust easily, absorb heat, harm the bark, and will allow the wired part of the tree to spring back into its original position.

In contrast to these wires, copper wire is soft and easy to bend and stretch. Being soft, it will not injure bark. Nor is there any danger that copper wire will spring back into itsoriginal position, but will stay in place for years. Moreover, the same wire can be used repeatedly.

Copper wire is undoubtedly the most suitable wire for the job, but it is also the most expensive, and

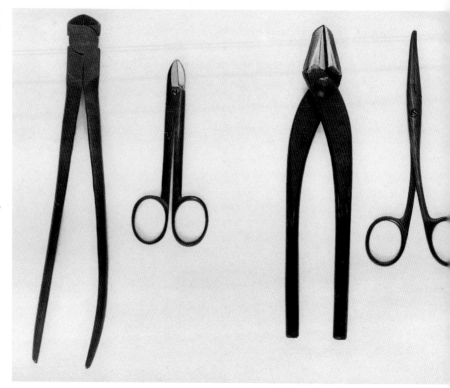

Left to right: Root cutter, nail-clipper for cutting fine wire, pincers for bending thick wire, and light pincers for thin wire.

develops poisonous verdigris when it rusts. It is advisable to keep on hand seven or eight different thicknesses of copper wiring, varying from 5.16 mm (¼ inch) to 0.56 mm (1/32 inch), as different thicknesses are required for different tasks. The 5.16 mm (¼ inch) wire is useful for bending trunks with a circumference of about 6 cm (24 inches), whereas the 0.56 mm (1/32 inch) wire is good for stretching or bending the thin, fine twigs of trees such as Shimpaku (Chinese Juniper) and Keyaki (Zelkova).

You will find, however, that the wire you will use most often is the medium-thickness wire, which ranges from 2.76 mm (⅛ inch) to 1.65 mm (1/16 inch). Generally a single piece of wire is used, but two or three thinner wires can be wound together for greater strength to take the place of thicker wire.

Copper wire has the property of hardening as soon as it comes in contact with moisture. So, when using copper wire, it is best to work near some source of heat, such as a small fire or a heater. This will rid the wire of moisture and soften it.

Once softened, the copper wire should be wound onto a spool for greater convenience in later use. Store your copper wire in a dry place. If you are re-using copper wire, you should again follow this procedure – that is, heat the wire so that you can remove all the twists remaining from the previous use, then wind it onto a spool. If you re-use wire it will absorb moisture again and stay in place just as well as new wire.

Paper tape

In some instances, if the copper wire could harm the tree, it is best to wrap paper tape around the wire before using it. This will also stop the wire from rusting, thus preventing the formation of poisonous verdigris.

Firstly, copper wire can be harmful due to its property as a good conductor of heat. In summer, for instance, it can reach a temperature of up to 100°F (38°C) just through the conduction of heat from the atmosphere. When it has been used to arrange branches, wire at such temperatures can easily burn the tree. This is particularly true in the case of species such as Sugi (Japanese Cedar), Momiji (Japanese Maple), Tō-Kaede (Trident Maple), and Keyaki (Zelkova), which have tender bark, and with young twigs in other trees. Secondly, if copper wire has been used to bend a branch at a very sharp angle, the wire can cut into the branch and damage it. Sometimes it can even cause the branch to break or wither. Paper tape will help prevent both these problems.

Raffia

Raffia is used to protect the tree from the wire. It should be applied horizontally, or both horizontally and vertically, to the trunk or branch that is to be bent. The wire is then applied over the raffia. If just one wrapping of raffia is not sufficient, then one to three pieces of thick copper wire should be placed inside the branch to be bent, and then wrapped with a double layer of raffia arranged both horizontally and vertically.

Raffia isn't necessary for young twigs that are being arranged by wiring, but should be used with trees that are particularly fragile or that have soft bark which is easily scarred, such as Nishiki-Matsu (a variety of Japanese Black Pine), Momiji (Japanese Maple) and Tō-Kaede (Trident Maple). It is also necessary when arranging the trunk or thick branches of a tree, or when dealing with trees whose bark might be scraped off, such as Goyō-Matsu (Five-Needled Pine).

Covering

When applying wire to a tree with soft bark, or when

How to wrap paper-tape around copper wire

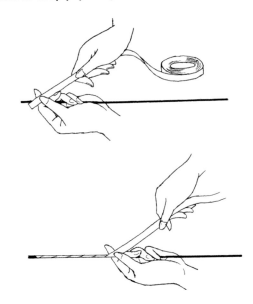

Three ways of wrapping raffia
The arrow shows the direction in which the tree is to be bent.

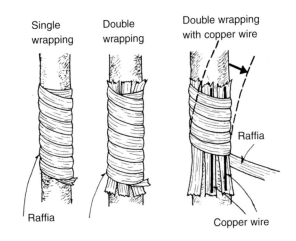

Single wrapping

Double wrapping

Double wrapping with copper wire

Raffia

Raffia

Raffia

Copper wire

How to use coverings

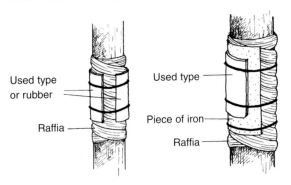

Used type or rubber

Used type

Raffia

Piece of iron

Raffia

using a lever to bend an old trunk or thick branch that is not pliable, it is best to protect the tree with some kind of covering; raffia will not suffice. Used tires, rubber hose, or sheet iron may be used as a covering. These materials should be cut into suitable sizes and wrapped with raffia. Use a covering wherever you want to create a sharp bend, or where a lever is to be applied to lighten the pressure.

Adhesive Plaster or Wax Cloth for Grafting

Adhesive plaster or wax cloth is used to prevent decay and hasten the healing process. It is applied to places where a cut has been made in the trunk or in a thick branch.

Above is a brief explanation of the use of various tools and materials used in arranging the branches of a bonsai. However, for a beginner who is trying to make a bonsai from a young tree, a cutting, or a grafted tree, you really just need two or three varieties of copper wire of medium thickness, some paper tape, raffia, and a pair of shears for cutting wood.

When to arrange by wiring

The appropriate time to arrange by wiring varies between species and climates. In the case of new twigs—that is, twigs that sprouted in the spring of the same year—the proper time is when the leaves are maturing and the growth of the twig has slowed down. The same goes for branches and trunks of trees aged between two and five years.

This is because at this time the circulation of the sap is very active, making the branches and trunks resilient and easier to work with. When a branch is bent in the desired direction during this time, there is little danger of damaging the tree and, as time goes by, the branch will assume the desired shape.

However, in the case of trees such as Kuro-Matsu (Japanese Black Pine) and Goyō-Matsu (Five-Needled Pine) in which the circulation of sap begins in early spring, arranging by wiring should be done a little earlier.

In contrast to the above, trunks and thick branches that are several years old should be wired sometime between the time when sap starts to circulate in spring and when the buds begin to develop. This may not seem like the best time for such a major undertaking, as it is then that branches and trunks tend to break easily and the tree itself is not very strong. But it is a time of year when bonsai-growers are comparatively free from the general care of their plant, so they can concentrate on such a major task. It also allows major operations to be performed without endangering the new buds. And, if sufficient care is exercised after the operation, there is no harm in choosing this time.

Preparation for arranging by wiring

To prepare a tree for wiring, you will need to give it adequate fertilizer for a year in advance. If it has received sufficient fertilizer, it should be supple, which will facilitate work and lessen the chances of injury. The tree will also be able to withstand much more stress than it otherwise would.

But don't give it too much water. If a tree is watered too much prior to arranging its branches by wiring, the trunk and branches will become hard and difficult to bend. It is therefore best to avoid wateringfor a day or two before wiring; the soil in the container should be dry.

For best results, have all the necessary tools on hand, and make sure your cutting tools are sharp.

The operation should be performed indoors where there is plenty of light, but no direct sunlight. A chair and a low table are needed, so that the work can be done while seated. A revolving table can be very handy for this type of work.

Determining the front and back of your bonsai

Some bonsai are beautiful when viewed from any side or angle, but such trees are very rare. Most have one side from which they are intended to be seen. The side that presents the most pleasing view—due to the way the roots grow, the shape of the trunk, the condition of the bark or foliage,or whatever is the most striking feature of your tree—should be made the front of the bonsai. The opposite side, then, will be the back. The terminal, or topmost point, of the tree should incline forward slightly, as this is the proper position for all bonsai. Once the front has been determined, your bonsai should always be placed so that it can be viewed from that side.

To determine which side is the front of your bonsai, you should place it on a table so that the middle of the tree is at eye-level. Then gradually turn your tree to find which side is the most beautiful. When a tree is to be planted in a container, the same procedure should be followed with the container, so that the front of the container and the front of the plant will match. This way, both the plant and the container can be viewed from the side that looks best.

The front and back of a
bonsai Toshō (Needle
Juniper).

(Front)

(Back)

Determining the shape of the tree

Part of the charm of bonsai is the fact that no two are alike. However, there are certain general types which are classified as follows:

Chokkan (formal straight trunk) A single tree with a straight trunk.

Sha-kan (slanting trunk) A single tree with a slanting trunk.

Moyō-gi (informal trunk) A single tree having a crooked trunk.

Sō-kan (twin trunks) A tree whose trunk is divided into two trunks near the roots, so that two trunks, one thick, the other thin, grow in parallel to one another. The Sankan is divided into three and the gokan into five.

Kengai (cascade tree) A single tree whose branches hang down in one direction.

Han-Kengai (semi-cascade tree) A single tree with a leaning trunk and thick branches that hang down in one direction.

Kabu-dachi (clumped trees) A tree that divides into several trunks near the roots, so that it appears to be a group of trees.

Ne-tsuranari (connecting roots) Roots of trees are connected.

Yose-ue (group planting) Several trees planted together.

Ishi-zuke or Ishi-zuki (trees planted on a rock) A tree or trees planted on a rock or rocks.

Ban-kan (twisting trunk) A single tree with a twisting or gnarled trunk.

Ikada-buki (raft-shaped trees) Branches grow from a horizontal trunk as if multible trees were planted together.

There are good and bad things about each of these forms. The important thing is to determine at the outset which one you wish to adapt for your bonsai. This decision should be made after you have examined your tree closely from the front.

In making this decision, such factors as root growth, how the tree grows out of the ground, the size and condition of the trunk and branches, and the harmony between the branches and the trunk, should be kept in mind. Then try to visualize the form most suited to the tree. Once you have an image in mind, you can reshape the tree to match your vision by cutting off all unwanted branches and wiring those that remain to pull them into the required shapes or positions. If, as a beginner, you

have no idea where to begin such an enterprise but wish to give your tree a classical bonsai form, the safest place to begin is by bending the trunk in the opposite direction to the branch.

Chokkan (formal straight trunk)

Sha-kan (slanting trunk)

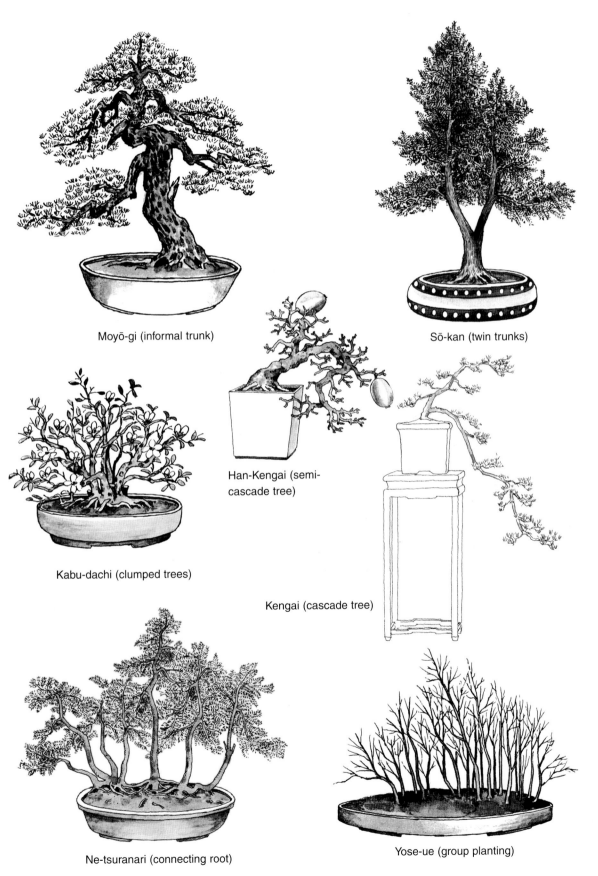

Moyō-gi (informal trunk)

Sō-kan (twin trunks)

Han-Kengai (semi-cascade tree)

Kabu-dachi (clumped trees)

Kengai (cascade tree)

Ne-tsuranari (connecting root)

Yose-ue (group planting)

Ishi-zuke or Ishi-zuki (trees planted on a rock)

Ban-kan (twisting trunk)

Ikada-buki (raft-shaped trees)

Unnecessary branches must be removed

Before wiring the branches of a tree, all unnecessary branches should first be cut off. This will improve the shape of the tree and make your work easier.

Unnecessary branches are defined as: (1) branches which have grown too dense; (2) withered branches; (3) branches which are growing in a direction contrary to one's image of the final shape of the bonsai, or a branch which slopes downward; (4) compartively thick branches that have grown out from the front of the tree.

How to remove the branches

Young trees

The best way to cut off branches varies with each tree, but in the case of young trees whose branches are to be arranged by wiring for the first time, attention must be paid to the following general points.

If the lowest remaining branch is on the right side, the next remaining branch must be on the left, and the third branch on the right. All other branches should be removed at their base as they are unnecessary—the first, second and third branches are the important branches. At the top, one thin terminal should be left. Or, if the lowest branch is on the left side, the second branch should be on the right. In other words, the important branches should alternate, and there should be one thin terminal branch at the top.

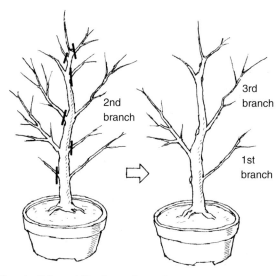

How to thin out the branches of a young tree

68

Thus the general shape of the tree is determined by the three branches and the terminal at the top.

Older trees

The same procedure can be applied to older trees that have been growing in the ground before being transplanted into containers. Although likely to have well-developed branches and foliage, they can still be arranged by wiring. In this case you may choose to leave more than three branches. Four or even five branches may be left, but they must still alternate from side to side. Other unnecessary branches should be cut off. For the top, one branch as close to the top of the tree as possible should be left. The places where thick branches have been cut off should be smoothed and covered either by adhesive plaster or by wax cloth.

How to shape the tree by bending the trunk sharply at the main branches

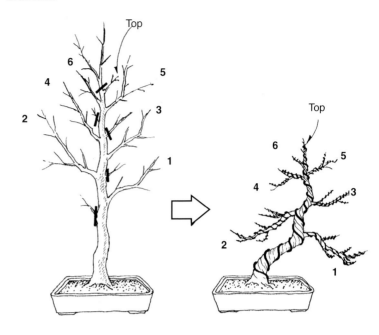

How to arrange the branches of a mature tree that was previously growing in the ground

How to arrange the branches of a tree obtained by layering

(Layering is a method of reproducing a plant by making its branches develop roots while they are still attached to the main plant. Once the roots are well-developed, the branch is subsequently cut off and planted as an individual plant.)

Trees that are already in the process of being arranged by wiring

To continue the process, it is only necessary to cut off branches that have withered or new branches that are unnecessary. The main branches and the top should already be mature. When doing this, remove the wire that remains from last year, beginning with the thinner wires near the edges of the tree and grad ually proceeding to the thicker wires.

You will probably find that the old wire is hard, especially the thicker wire, and may have cut into the bark in some places. Cut this wire with pincers so you can remove it without further damage to the bark.

Order of wiring

Before going into a detailed explanation of wiring, the order in which a tree is wired should be described. In the case of young trees: (1) start at the bottom of the trunk and gradually move upwards; (2) after wiring the trunk, wire the first branch from the base to the tip; (3) wire the first twig on the first branch, from base to tip, then the second twig on the same branch, and so on; (4) when wiring hasbeen completed on all the twigs on the first branch, repeat the process with the second branch; (5) proceed to the third branch; (6) lastly, begin at the bottom of the terminal and proceed to the tip.

In the case of older trees

This manner of wiring is satisfactory with young trees, but as older trees have more branches the process can become rather complicated. So, with older trees, simply start from wherever is easiest. Those branches which are more difficult may be left until last, and if you find a branch that is unusually difficult to wire, just leave it.

Wiring the trunk

Above are some examples of how to wire a tree. In the case of young trees which have not developed any special characteristics it may be necessary to wire the whole tree to give it the desired shape. While this is not easy, it is a delightful task which can give the bonsai-grower much satisfaction.

Since the wiring method varies considerably with the age of a tree, wiring of both a young tree and an older specimen will be described.

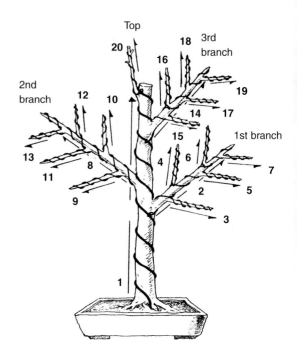

Showing the steps of wiring the branches
The wires should be applied in the order of the numbers and in the direction indicated by the arrow.

How to bend the trunk with your hands

Wiring a young trunk

First place the container on a table. Then, bearing in mind the shape you wish to give your tree, apply both hands to the part of the tree that requires either bending or straightening, beginning with the lower part, and bend the trunk gently several times. After this, making sure that the trunk can be bent as far as you wish, proceed with the wiring.

The copper wire you use on the trunk should be thick enough to prevent the trunk from springing back into its original position. In trees that have hard bark, like pines, the wire may be applied directly to the bark. But for trees that have soft bark, like Momiji (Japanese Maple), Tō-Kaede (Trident Maple), Keyaki (Zelkova), Ume-modoki (*Ilex serrata* var. Sieboldii), and Sugi (Japanese Cedar), first wrap the wire in paper tape.

In the case of Satsuki (Satsuki Azalea), which has such soft bark that wire cuts into it even when applied over paper tape, raffia should be wound around the places that will be wired.

Before wiring the trunk, firmly secure the end of the wire. The best way to do this is to bury the end so that it reaches right to the bottom of the container. As the inside of the container is filled with the root system, the wire will not easily be pulled out. This is very important, because if the wire is not properly secured wiring will not be effective.

However, if the area to be wired is far above the base of the trunk, you don't need wire going all the way up the trunk. You will therefore need to secure the wire elsewhere than at the base of the trunk. In this case, apply a covering, as described above, to the area. Then you will be able to fasten the wire

Showing how wire wrapped with paper is thrust to the bottom of the container beside the trunk.

securely around the covering without damaging the tree's bark, and start wiring from there. If it is not possible to use a covering for some reason, secure the wire by tying it to one of the main branches.

After the wire is fastened, cut it to a length about 9 to 15 cm (3½ to 6 inches) longer than the entire length of the trunk. This extra length is necessary to

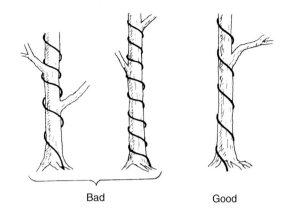

Bad   Good

Technique of applying the wires
When bending, apply constant pressure with the thumb.

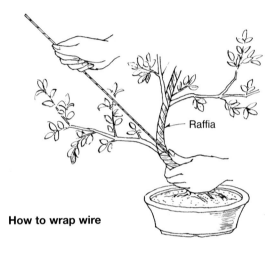

Raffia

How to wrap wire

allow for winding the wire; the more winding there is to be done, the more extra wire you will need to allow.

But take care not to wind the wire too closely because if you do this the wire will not hold and you'll end up using an excessive amount.

Wind the wire slowly, using one hand. As you wind, use the thumb of the other hand to press the wire against the bark. It should be neither too loose nor too tight. The hand that is winding the wire should not release it midway or the tension in the wire will be affected and some parts of the wire will be wound tightly and other parts will be wound loosely, with the result that the wire will not hold.

As you wind the wire, be careful not to break any branches. In places where you want to bend or straighten the trunk sharply, the wire should be

Wrap wire so that it will come on the outside of the place to be bent sharply.

71

Arranging the branches of a Toshō (Needle Juniper) which was wired last year. Wrap the wire so that is on the outside of the place to be bent sharply.

wound so that it lies on the outside of the bend (see illustration). This will make the wire hold better. When you have finished wiring an area, bend the end of the wire with pliers, then cut it with pincers after making sure that the tree will not spring back into its original position.

After the wire is wound, the trunk is ready to be bent or straightened. Here too, begin at the bottom of the tree, near the roots.

Grasp the trunk with both hands, one a little above the place that is to be bent and one a little below it. Press your thumbs against the trunk, and bend it to the desired position. When doing this, be sure to bend the trunk in the same direction that the

wire winds, twisting it slightly with the wire. This will make the wire take better effect. In the case of trees that snap easily, it is enough merely to bend the trunk. When the twists have been straightened (see illustration), the work of applying wires to the tree is complete.

Wiring a 6—10 year-old tree

First make sure that the trunk will not move by fastening it to the container with twine. Then place the container on your table, and begin to work on the tree according to your envisaged shape of the plant. Always begin with the lower part of the trunk.

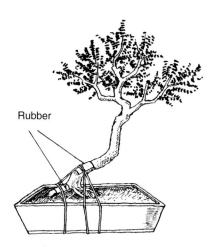

Rubber

Fasten the base of the trunk so that the tree will not move.

How to cut the trunk using a root-cutter.

72

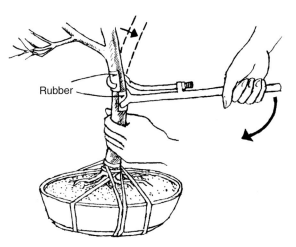

Rubber

Technique of bending the trunk with a lever.

Unlike the young trees described above, the trunk of an older tree may be too thick and hard to bend by hand. Before you can wire a tree like this, you will probably need to use pruning shears or a lever to make bending easier.

Pruning shears are a good tool to use when you want to bend the trunk of your tree to an acute angle. If you make one or two cuts vertically where you want the trunk to bend, you will be able to bend it easily. The disadvantage of this method is that it leaves a wound on the trunk. It is therefore not suitable for trees in which such injuries are slow to heal, but may be used for Kuro-Matsu (Japanese Black Pine), Aka-Ezo-Matsu (Saghalien Spruce), and other species in which wounds heal quickly.

There are three advantages to using a lever to arrange branches: it will not injure the trunk or thick branches of a tree; it is suitable for bending and straightening branches; and it is simple and durably made. I devised this instrument myself, based upon several, years experience, especially for use by bonsai growers.

As shown in the illustration, first apply a piece of rubber or tyre a little above or below the place that is to be bent. Then lock the lever. Next, apply a similar covering to the inside of the place to be bent. Apply the end of the lever and gently pull the handle and bend the trunk to the desired position. Repeat this two or three times until the trunk can be bent easily. Then remove the lever.

When you want to straighten a trunk that is bent, the process is practically the same. Use two levers, one a little above and the other a little below the place to be straightened, pull both handles gently upward at the same time, and stop when the trunk has become straight. Repeat the process two or three times until the trunk can be bent easily, then remove the levers.

After making the trunk more flexible by this means, wire can be applied. In the case of trees with easily damaged bark, wrap one or two layers of raffia around the tree before wiring. The wire itself should be covered with paper tape.

The manner of winding the wires is similar to the manner used in the case of young trees. If you are using two or three thin wires instead of one thick wire, be careful not to tangle the wires. Wind them so that they will lie side by side, parallel to one another, and adhere closely to the bark.

After winding the wires, apply the lever again in the same manner as before and you will be able to bend the trunk to the desired position. Lastly, remove the lever.

How to apply wire to branches

Branches that grow upwards are characteristic of strong young trees, and create an impression of vitality. The vitality of these branches is lost, however, when they are pulled down to a horizontal

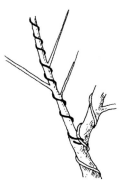

How to secure the wire to be applied to a branch.

position or lower. Such branches, as are growing straight out or down, are characteristic of old trees that are past their prime and are therefore an undesirable characteristic in bonsai. This is something that all bonsai-growers must keep in mind when wiring the branches of their bonsai.

Start with the first branch up from the base of the tree. Use wire that is thinner than that used for the trunk, but which is still thick enough to prevent the arranged branch from springing back into its original position. In the case of trees that snap easily or those whose bark is easily injured, first wind raffia around the branches and paper tape around the wires.

The best way to apply the wire depends on such factors as how old the tree is and whether the branches are thick or thin. In general, however, thick branches are wired the same way as the trunk. The method for wiring thin branches and twigs is described next.

How to wire the branches of young tree

First fasten the wire by tying it to the trunk or to the wiring on the trunk. If there is a withered branch near the first branch, the wire may be fastened to that. In any case, fasten the wire so that it will not move. Once it has been fastened securely, cut the wire so that it is about 3–9 cm (1¼–3½ inches) longer than the branch.

Then wind the wire around the branch, working from the base to the end. It should be wound tightly enough to lie close to the bark. Take care not to break any small twigs in the process. Once you reach the tip of the branch, wind the end of the wire twice round the tip and fasten it so that it will not spring back. Cut off the excess wire with a pair of pincers.

Sometimes a branch or the trunk may fork into two smaller branches. When this happens, the only effective way to wire the two forking branches is with a single piece of wire (see illustration). So when you begin, make the wire long enough for both branches. Fasten the wire in the middle of the fork then wind the wire clockwise up one branch and counter-clockwise up the other.

After attaching the wire, bend the main branch, starting at the base. This should be done with various factors in mind, such as the total appearance of the tree, and the condition of the growth of the smaller branches. Elements such as making the upper part of the tree balance with the lower, the left with the right, and the larger branches with the

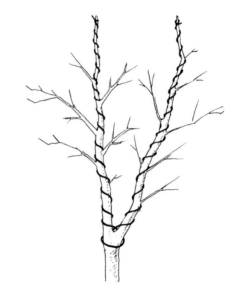

How to apply wire to forked branches.

Ensure that the tips of small branches point upwards.

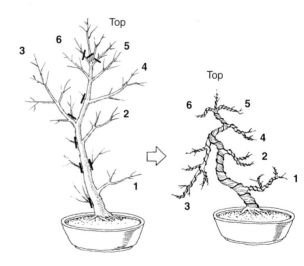

Comparing the appearance of the tree before and after its branches have been arranged by wiring.

74

smaller, should be considered so that the branches look like the lower branches on an old tree. Bending by hand, without special instruments, should be possible in the case of young trees and trees that are about ten years old. Use both hands when bending the branches. Just remember that when bending a branch, strength should be applied not only with the finger-tips but with the thumbs as well.

After wiring the first main branch, the next step is to wire the small branches or twigs growing off the main branch, moving gradually from the base of the main branch to the end.

The following three points should be borne in mind while this operation is being performed:

1. Use a thinner wire than that used for the main branch. Fasten one end securely to the wire that is wrapped around the main branch.

2. After wiring all the small branches of a larger branch, position them carefully so that they do not overlap. Space them evenly so that each will receive the same amount of sunlight.

3. Take care that the ends of the small branches do not point downwards as this is not good for the tree and may even cause the branches to wither. Make sure that the tips are slightly raised.

Follow this same procedure with the second and third branches, moving gradually toward the top of the tree.

Sometimes you may want to shape a branch to fill an area of the tree that looks rather bare. If this is the case, you can solve the problem either by choosing a branch that is near the bare area and changing its direction, or by pulling a branch over into position.

When doing this, if you want to bend a branch to the right, you must wind the wire to the right, and if you want it bent to the left, you must wind the wire

to the left. This will enable you to bend the branch at a sharp angle. Otherwise the wiring will be ineffective and the branch could be damaged.

In this operation, cover the branch that you want to bend with raffia and wrap the wire with paper tape. Above all, take great care that the final placement of the branch will not look unnatural or awkward.

How to apply wire to a new shoot

The time to wire new shoots is when their leaves have more or less matured and the bark at the base of the twigs has begun to harden.

If wiring is done at this time, the new shoots will be resilient enough to allow wiring to be done with reasonable ease and without causing too much damage.

Wiring is very effective on young shoots as it retards the growth of the shoot and takes effect almost immediately as the twigs harden. You will find that after only two or three months the branches will be properly arranged.

Hence wiring young shoots has the effect not only of checking unwanted growth, but also of giving the tree the desired shape.

When wiring branches, first remove any unnecessary shoots, then thin out patches where the shoots may be too dense. Cut the shoots off at the base.

Of the new shoots that are left, only wire those that need it—that is, those which may grow in a fashion contrary to the desired shape of the tree.

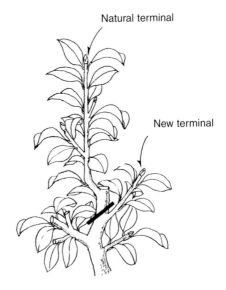

Natural terminal

New terminal

How to make a new terminal.

How to apply wire to a new twig.

As new shoots have soft bark which may be harmed by the wire, wrap the wire with paper tape. No special tools are needed. Bend the twig by hand two or three times to the desired angle or position. Once the twig is moving fairly flexibly in the desired direction, fasten one end of your piece of wire and wind the other end around the twig, starting at the base.

Apply the same technique as was used on the main branches, taking care not to tear off any leaves in the process.

After winding the wire around the twig, bend the twig to the desired position and then nip the tips of the buds on the new twigs. But be careful not to have the entire branch pointing downwards or it will lose its vitality; to prevent this, keep the very tip raised.

Wiring the terminal

After you have wired all the branches, you should wire the terminal so that it points upwards. In a bonsai, the terminal, or topmost point of the tree, is actually a branch that has been wired into shape to replace the natural terminal. If the natural terminal remained, the tree would continue to grow taller, a tendency that is not desired in a bonsai. Moreover, as the energy of the tree is usually focussed on its growing taller, the presence of the natural terminal can result in lower branches withering, and the tree generally becoming difficult to handle. Accordingly, with most bonsai, the trunk is cut off at about the middle, and the terminal of a branch is raised instead.

Whether a tree is still growing, so no terminal is obvious as yet, or whether it has a terminal that is taller than is ideal, a new terminal must be created. To do this, choose a small branch with good leaves that occurs at a point on the tree that is about as high as you wish your tree to grow, and cut off all the branches growing above it (see illustration). Then wire the branch which is to be the new terminal. The wiring should be done from below so that the terminal will stand up straight. The very tip of the terminal should incline slightly to the front of the tree.

Precautions to be taken when wiring

1. Remember that wiring a tree is an irritation to the plant, so take every step carefully.
2. When winding wire, do it in a single operation without winding the same place twice.
3. When bending a branch after it has been wired, twist it slightly in the same direction as that in which the wire is wound. Never twist it in the opposite direction.
4. If you can't obtain the desired shape of the tree purely by wiring, use the technique called suspending the branches. If you use this technique on a branch that is to be arranged at an acute angle, apply raffia and also pieces of rubber where there will be contact with the wire.
5. Start by wiring a tree that is easy to handle. After mastering the technique, proceed to more difficult trees.

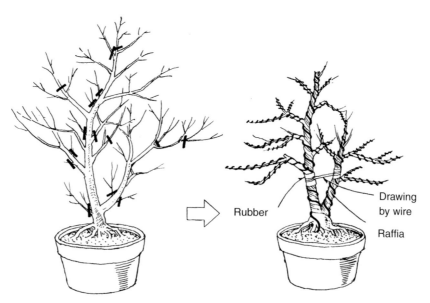

Rubber

Drawing by wire

Raffia

Example of a tree whose branches have been arranged by combining the two methods of wiring and suspending.

Left to right: Miniature, small and large bonsai.

Wiring and the height of bonsai

When you have finished wiring your tree, the trunk and branches will be bent. Consequently, your bonsai will be shorter than it was originally. How much shorter it is will depend on the degree of curvature of the trunk and branches. This miniaturisation is a major characteristic of bonsai, and is therefore a welcome side-effect of wiring. But what is the proper height of a bonsai? This depends on such factors as the grower's taste and where the bonsai is grown, but from the point of view of care and enjoyment, the proper height should be from 45 to 55 cm (16⅕ to 10⅕ inches). Trees that exceed this height arecalled large bonsai, and those which are smaller are called small bonsai.

If a tree is shorter than 12 cm (5 inches), it is called a miniature bonsai. However, such extra-small bonsai are very difficult to care for properly, and cannot give the bonsai-grower the true delight that real bonsai offer.

How to care for your bonsai after it has been arranged by wiring

As wiring is a highly stressful process for a plant, it must be allowed to rest after the procedure. For this, place the container where it is completely sheltered from wind and direct sunlight. Give it plenty of water, pouring it over the entire plant. Do this once or twice a day for some time after wiring. After a suitable rest period, return your tree to its outdoor shelf.

The period of rest that a bonsai needs depends on the extent of its wiring

Ordinarily, three to four days will be enough time, but a tree that has been subjected to a major operation needs a rest-period of about a week. During this time, do not give the tree any fertilizer or insecticide. After the bonsai has been restored to its outdoor shelf, fertilizer can again be applied.

How long does it take for a branch to bend permanently after it has been arranged by wiring? With proper wiring, young twigs and thin branches will bend in about two to three months. Thicker branches take from three to four months. Sometimes one has to wait for more than a year before the branch acquires a permanent bend.

If the wires do not produce the desired results, what should be done? If, for instance, the wires cut into the bark, they should be removed at once. If wiring has had no effect on the tree, either the method was wrong, or the tree simply does not bend easily. In either case, try again the following year.

Arranging the branches by wiring is a difficult technique, but if you do it yourself you will be sure to enjoy the pleasure of bonsai-growing, even if you are not always successful.

SOME FINER POINTS
OF CARE

Love your bonsai!

Bonsai is the art of planting a tree in a container, then lavishing attention on it so that one day you will be able to enjoy your own miniature replica of beautiful natural scenery. It is vital, therefore, to watch over your bonsai with unfailing affection. Any person who wishes to grow bonsai should spare at least ten to twenty minutes per day, either in the morning or in the evening, to care for their plant. Without such effort, successful bonsai growing can hardly be expected.

If you truly love your bonsai, you will not fail to take note of such things as the level of moisture in the soil, the condition of the buds, the color of the leaves, and the growth of the new shoots, all of which are indicators for the amount of fertilizer required, the presence of insects or disease, and the state of the flowers, fruits, leaves, and roots. Such vigilance and care will allow you to take appropriate action the moment a problem arises.

It is impossible to overstate the importance of watering your bonsai whenever the soil becomes dry, and of keeping insects at bay. The very first step in bonsai management is to watch over one's plant daily and with genuine affection, so that if anything is wrong the appropriate countermeasure can be taken immediately.

Transplanting

Purpose
The purpose of transplanting is to change the soil in the container before the container becomes filled with the plant's root system, which will prevent the soil from functioning properly. It also gives new roots a chance to develop.

When to transplant
The time it takes for a tree's root system to fill its container depends on such things as what type of tree it is, how fast it grows, its stage of growth, the type and amount of fertilizer it is given, its soil mixture, and so on.

In general, however, a tree in the growing stage should be transplanted once a year, while a mature tree should be transplanted once every two or three years. Pines are exceptions, and only need transplanting once every four to five years. For other types of trees, the time for transplanting is shown in the chart at the end of the book.

Transplanting soil and method
The subjects of soil composition and how to transplant a bonsai have been discussed in the Introduction to Bonsai Growing (page 41).

When transplanting, remove the old soil as thoroughly as possible, and prune the ends of the fine roots. Then remove any unwanted branches. Finally, plant the tree firmly in a new container that has good drainage.

The container for transplanting
When transplanting a tree that has a definite shape, you need to select a container carefully, so that its shape and color will suit the tree. This will ensure the enjoyment of the container as well as the plant.

Aka-Ezo-Matsu, (Saghalien Spruce) being transplanted from a pot for growing into a Bonsai container.

Examples of containers that are traditionally used for certain types of plants:

For evergreen, needle-leafed trees, use containers of red earthenware, dark grey earthenware, violet earthenware, or containers of imported Chinese earthenware.

For evergreen flowering trees, use grey containers.

For deciduous flowering trees, use celadon porcelain containers if the flowers are white or yellow, and use grey ones if the flowers are red.

For deciduous trees with autumn-tinted leaves, use celadon porcelain, or grey or white earthenware.

For deciduous trees with fruits, use white earthenware, white cochin-china, or violet earthenware.

Where to put bonsai and the question of fertilizer application

This subject has already been discussed in the section on trees used for practise. The important thing to remember is that, after transplanting, a plant has to be treated with extra care until its roots develop. When its roots have developed, the plant may be placed on an outdoor shelf, but it must be given plenty of water and not allowed to dry out. Weak fertilizer should be given whenever the plant needs it.

A tree in the growing stage should be given proper care so that it will take on a pleasing shape; don't try to hasten the bearing of flowers or fruits, but concentrate instead on growing a healthy tree. Apply sufficient fertilizer during the growing season. Give the trunk and branches a chance to grow strong and sturdy, and let the tree assume a definite shape. In the case of trees that bear flowers or fruit, the application of reasonably large quantities of fertilizer containing phosphate or potassium will stimulate blossoming and fruit-bearing. The ideal result of fertilizer application is to prolong the enjoyment of flowers and fruits for as long as possible.

Nipping the buds and arranging by wiring

As a tree gets older, it tends to sprout more and more new buds. To prevent the ensuing growth of a dense profusion of branches, thin the buds out by nipping them as soon as possible. Buds that appear in pairs on opposite sides of the branch or trunk should be nipped to leave alternate buds. Once the unwanted buds have been removed, every care should be taken to ensure the healthy development of those that remain.

To ensure the growth of fine, dense branch-tips, nipping should be repeated to increase the number of sprouting buds. However, if the tree has flowers on its new twigs or if its branches are in danger of withering in winter as a result of nipping, bud-nipping should be postponed until after the new shoots have grown long and begun to swell or harden. Then the tips of the more energetic new shoots should be nipped.

Some new shoots may grow with unexpected vigour, with the result that the internodes become too large. This, in turn, would cause a great number of large leaves to grow, making it dificult for air to flow through the plant, and making the bonsai look cluttered and unkempt. Maple trees (Kaede), in particular, have this tendency. Such trees should be arranged by wiring, as this will retard the growth of the shoots and retain the shape of the tree. These wires must be removed in autumn or they will cut into the bark.

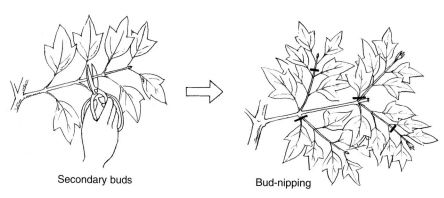

Secondary buds

Bud-nipping

How to prune the shoots of trees like Tō-Kaede (Trident Maple) and Momiji (Japanese Maple). If trees have shoots that grow in opposite pairs, prune them alternately.

Control of insects and disease

The infestation of insects and disease is common with bonsai. In unfavorable conditions—for instance where there is a lack of sunlight or air circulation or a shortage of plant nutrition—poor growth is inevitable. Accordingly, preventative measures should be taken. Spray your plant regularly with water in winter and in spring just before the buds come out, then at budding time in spring, and in the hot dry weather of early summer when outbreaks are common.

If an outbreak occurs, the infected part of the tree should either be cut off and burnt to prevent the infestation from spreading, and the insects caught and killed, or an effective insecticide should be applied.

Cutting the leaves

This technique is used to enhance the shape of the tree by creating soft, delicate and dense branches. It is suitable for use with species such as Momiji (Japanese Maple), Tō-Kaede (Trident Maple), Keyaki (Zelkova) and Nire-Keyaki (Chinese Elm).

Weak branch

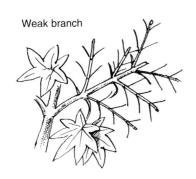

Healthy branch

How to cut the leaves of Momiji (Japanese Maple).

How to cut the leaves

Using a pair of specially-made light shears, cut the leaves about two months after transplanting, when the leaves on the new twigs have matured. Start at the top of the tree and work down. There are various ways to make the cut, depending on the variety of tree and the health of the branch. In the case of Momiji (Japanese Maple) or Tō-Kaede (Trident Maple), the leaves are cut from about the middle of the leaf stalk (see illustration).

However, even in these species, if an important branch is not thriving it is best either to leave its leaves uncut or, if the leaves have to be cut, only to cut the very tips off the leaves.

In the case of Keyaki (Zelkova) or Nire-Keyaki (Chinese Elm), the leaves are far smaller and more numerous than in the case of the maple, so cutting every leaf is a tedious task. With such species, first use shears to cut off all the unnecessary tips of the branches, then remove the remaining leaves either with shears or by hand.

Momiji (Japanese Maple) ten days after its leaves have been cut.

Do not cut the leaves of a weakened tree. Leaf-cutting is a drastic operation for a tree, and should be avoided if your tree looks at all unhealthy. Again, before the leaves of any tree are cut, plenty of fertilizer should be applied in order to strengthen the tree. This is a precautionary measure to ensure that the tree will not suffer from the leaf-cutting.

After cutting its leaves, water your tree well and put it on an outdoor shelf so that it will get plenty of sunlight. Then water it two to three times a day to induce the buds to sprout. If this is too much trouble, keep your plant indoors in a place with plenty of light, and sprinkle water on it once a day until the buds begin to appear. It can be taken outside after that.

After the buds have begun to appear, the plant should be sprinkled with water every day. A little liquid fertilizer can also be applied from time to time to help the tree recover its full strength. This technique will ensure the growth of smaller and denser leaves, and the tree will come to have branches of a delicate and graceful appearance.

More reasons not to put your bonsai on the ground

Ways to protect your bonsai from the cold, and from attacks of disease and insects were discussed on page 55 and page 57 respectively. Below we will cover simple countermeasures to prevent damage from two more common threats: wind, and domestic animals, such as cats and dogs.

Wind can cause considerable damage to bonsai. This is particularly true of bonsai that are placed on high tables or shelves. Despite this, it is not a good idea to place the containers directly on the ground as that could result in both the container and the leaves becoming muddy. In addition, earthworms could enter the container through the hole in the bottom and cause damage. Containers on the ground are also hard to care for properly. For instance, if they are placed on stones, bricks, tiles or concrete, the roots will suffer from the cold in winter, and the strong heat of summer can also harm the plant.

Accordingly, shelves or tables made of thick boards are the best place for your bonsai. But when placing the container on a shelf, take the precaution of tying it down to prevent it from being blown over by a strong wind.

Damage from domestic animals
Domestic animals are a nuisance to bonsai. Due to

the habit of dogs and cats of always urinating in the same place, never place bonsai on the ground.

Carving in order to conceal a scar

Bonsai should be free from scarring. A conspicuous scar will reduce its value as a bonsai considerably. So if a trunk is damaged by insects or disease, or is decayed or scarred, or if a branch shows a conspicuous scar, the damaged area can be concealed by a technique known as carving.

How carving is done
Carving should be done indoors during the plant's winter rest period. Tie the base of the trunk firmly to the container so that the plant cannot move. With a sharp carving knife, gradually carve out the decayed or withered part. Take care not to hurt any of the living part of the tree or its leaves.

Try to carve out the decayed part so that the hole you make looks like one of the natural hollows that is often found in old trees. Leave the hard core, and smooth over the surface of the carved area. Then, to prevent further decay, apply adhesive plaster or wax cloth to that area.

After carving, keep your bonsai in a warm room, and water it every day to stimulate its recovery and help the wound to heal.

If you feel it is necessary you may also give your bonsai some weak fertilizer. If the plant is taken care of in this manner, the area around the wound will begin to heal and in two or three years the scar will be almost invisible.

Some of the most graceful and dignified bonsai have *shari-kan*, or a weathered dead branch or trunk. Such branches are created by carving to give bonsai the appearance of a tree which has grown in a rugged environment under severe conditions. Rugged shapes and rough edges are prized by the Japanese, and adding such elements to your bonsai will enhance its appearance.

Carving a *jin*
When part of a tree trunk dies, and its bark falls off to expose whitened wood, this is called a *shari-kan*. A dead branch is called a *jin*. Owing to exposure to the elements, lightning, falling rocks, and other natural forces, limbs will break, or death will come to tree trunks. *Shari-kan* refers to a condition in which the bark and soft wood rot away, and the remaining hard portion turns white.

Various kinds of knives for carving the trunks or branches.

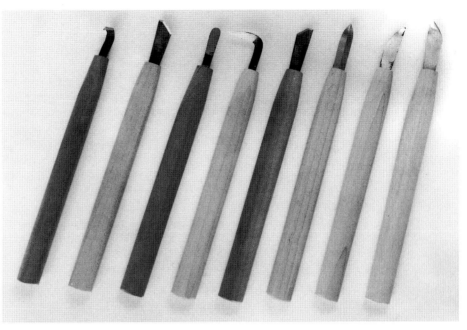

Toshō (Needle Juniper) featuring a *jin* (dead and weathered top).

How to make a Jin

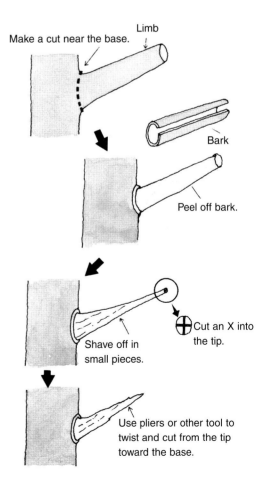

Make a cut near the base.

Limb

Bark

Peel off bark.

Shave off in small pieces.

Cut an X into the tip.

Use pliers or other tool to twist and cut from the tip toward the base.

Layering

Deciduous trees should be layered from early April through June. Temperatures of over 68°F (20°C) are needed for the trees to grow roots, so the best time is from late May through June.

Obtaining new plants by layering
Layering is the method used to propagate new plants by making the branches of the parent plant grow roots. After roots have developed, the branch is then severed from the tree and replanted as an individual plant. There are two different methods of layering: air layering and earth layering. Air layering is the best method for creating a bonsai from a branch which already exhibits the natural shape and curvature desirable in bonsai. First, wrap wire (#10 width)

once around the base of the chosen branch, making sure that the wire penetrates about half-way into the bark. Then water thoroughly, cover the area with a pack of sphagnum (moss), and tie up each end with a strong rope. As the branch grows larger, the wire will penetrate deeper into its bark, facilitating the growth of roots. Water twice a day, morning and evening. After one or two months, remove the sphagnum. If 4 or 5 roots have grown out of the area above where the sphagnum was placed, and those roots are white with reddish-black tips, then the layering has been successful. Sever the branch from the parent plant and replant immediately into a large bonsai container. At first only put it in direct sunlight for half the day. Once the plant is established, you will be able to leave it on your bonsai shelf in full sunlight for the whole day.

(1) Tie with two windings of wire.

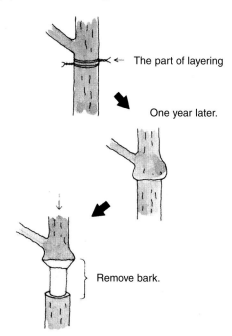

The part of layering

One year later.

Remove bark.

(2) Layering Toward stand.

For the Kengai Style

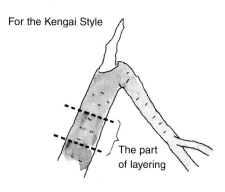

The part of layering

For the Kabu-Dachi Style

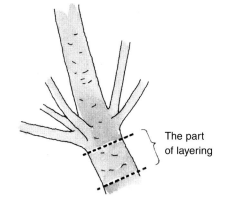

The part of layering

For the So-kan Style

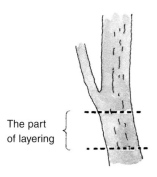

The part
of layering {

1

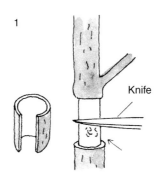

Knife

Peel off bark so that wood
can be slightly scraped off.

2

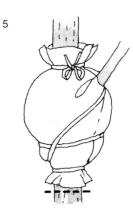

Wrap on wet sphagnum moss.

3

Cover sphagnum moss with
plastic, tie at top and bottom.

4

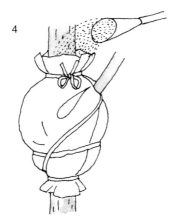

Be sure to water when moss dries.

5

Cut here, being careful
not to damage the roots.

6

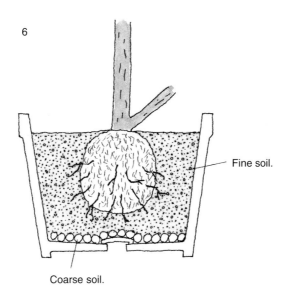

Fine soil.

Coarse soil.

GROWING SOME TYPICAL BONSAI

Needle-Leafed Evergreens

Kuro-Matsu (Japanese Black Pine)

Characteristics
This very hardy tree can live for hundreds of years, even in the confines of a container. As it ages, its trunk will thicken, its bark will become rough, and its branches vigorous. Its evergreen leaves, pointing toward the sky, are traditionally considered to be a masculine feature. The shape of the tree increases in elegant grandeur with age, and its beauty is indescribable. It is infinitely suitable for growing as bonsai. What is more, it is also easy to grow. As a tree that can be viewed with pleasure all year round, it is considered to belong to a class superior to all other types of trees.

Type of tree to use as bonsai
The best tree for this purpose is an old dwarfed tree that has aged in the ground rather than in a container. If you can find such a tree, its leaves should be small, dense, and beautiful. Those that also have hard and cracked bark are more highly valued. The best time to transplant it to a container is when the new buds begin to appear. Prune the large roots to suit the container, leaving as much soil attached to the root system as possible. Then prune the branches, and plant the tree in the garden for a year or two, applying large amounts of fertilizer to develop its fine roots. Dig the plant out again in spring just before the buds come out, and plant it firmly in an unglazed pot, using soil containing 20 to 30% coarse sand to facilitate water drainage.

Care
Put the container where it will get plenty of sunlight and air all year round. Sea breezes will do it no harm, unlike dust or the exhaust fumes from traffic. Water the tree whenever the surface of the soil in the container becomes dry. In very hot weather, syringe the leaves. For fertilizer, use only rapeseed cake. After the roots are fully developed, deposit two or three tablespoonfuls of powdered or dried fertilizer about three times a year. A white myceloid membrane that forms at the bottom of the container is an indication that the pine is growing vigorously.

Nipping
The buds should be nipped rather closely, varying, however, with the length of the new shoots. New shoots blossom between April and May. Before they actually come into bloom, nip the strong buds at the base and the weaker buds just above the base. After about a month or so, two to three secondary shoots will appear from the base of the shoots that were nipped. There is no need to nip these secondary shoots, as they do not grow very long. By nipping the primary shoots and allowing the secondary shoots to grow, the branches and leaves will become smaller, which is what you want when growing bonsai.

Maintenance and pest control
The leaves of Kuro-Matsu generally last for two years, but as they grow old they become dusty and unsightly. For this reason it is best to tear the old leaves off after the lingering heat of summer is over. While a tree is in the growing stage, infestations by red spiders, caterpillars and wooly aphids are common. These should be controlled with insecticides.

Arranging the branches by wiring
The best time to do this is in spring before the buds come out. In general, wires may be used without any wrapping, but if you want to bend the trunk or a thick branch at an acute angle and are concerned that you may damage the bark in the process, just wrap some raffia around the place which is to be bent.

Kuro-Matsu (Japanese Black Pine)

Carving

If you scar the tree by cutting the trunk or a thick branch, you should carve the area so that it will look like a natural flaw in the bark. Carving is best done indoors in the winter while the plant is dormant.

If you have a withered branch at the top of your tree, this can be turned into a feature by peeling off the bark and removing the soft wood part, resulting in a *jin*, or weathered dead top. To create a *jin*, when you cut off a withered branch or portion of trunk from a tree, leave 2 or 3 cm (⅔ or 1¼ inches) of it in

tact. Then strip the bark from this remaining stump of branch or trunk and the resulting feature will add character to your bonsai.

Transplanting

At first, your tree should be transplanted every three years, but after the initial period, transplant every four or five years. The time to transplant is when new buds appear. Black Pines should be planted in a soil comprised of red clay and coarse sand mixed in the proportion of 7 : 3 respectively.

Nishiki-Matsu (Japanese Black Pine) with extraordinarily developed cork-tissue.

Other trees that may be treated in the same way as Kuro-Matsu

There are many varieties of Kuro-Matsu. One variety is Nishiki-Matsu (Japanese Black Pine). Its bark is very rough and cracked like the back of a turtle. Aka-Matsu (Japanese Red Pine) is an entirely different species, though it resembles Kuro-Matsu. Its bark is finer, smoother and reddish in color. Its leaves are also finer and softer and the shape of the tree is characteristically feminine.

Both these trees can be grown as bonsai in the same way as Kuro-Matsu. In the case of Nishiki-Matsu, however, one should start with a grafted tree or a cutting.

Goyō-Matsu (Five-Needled Pine)

Characteristics

As with Kuro-Matsu (Japanese Black Pine), this hardy tree can live for hundreds of years in a container. Although it is a slow-growing tree, its trunk will gradually thicken and the branches become numerous. The bark resembles that of Aka-Matsu (Japanese Red Pine) but is finer. It has short leaves which grow in clusters of five, are evergreen and have a white line in them. The shape of the tree is graceful and feminine, and as the tree ages, its dignity increases. It is a beautiful tree that lends itself particularly to growing as a bonsai due to the various shapes it can be made to take. It has the additional advantage of maintaining a given shape for several years. Together with Kuro-Matsu, it is counted among the best trees to grow as bonsai.

Varieties

Different varieties of Goyō-Matsu grow in different regions of Japan. Some have thick, coarse bark, while others have a bark that is thin and fine. Some varieties have long, thick, curved needles, while others have short, thin, straight ones. The needles can also vary in color, such as silver and gold, dark and pale. One variety, which grows in alpine areas, has a trunk that crawls along the ground, and for this reason it is called Hai-Matsu (Dwarf Stone Pine).

Of these, the one best suited for growing as bonsai has short, small, and dense leaves, delicate branches with short internodes, thick, rough bark. The dwarf Yatsubusa-Shō Goyō-Matsu (Five-Needled Pine with Eight Clusters) is especially ideal, having short dense leaves and branches. It is dwarfed in nature and is much prized by bonsai-growers. This plant is ideal for growing as a miniature bonsai.

Goyō-Matsu (Five-Needled Pine), with layering applied.

Type of tree to use as bonsai

In the case of Yatsubusa-Shō Goyō-Matsu (Five-Needled Pine with Eight Clusters), it is best to begin with a cutting or a grafted tree. But the case of the other kinds of Goyō-Matsu, use an old tree of a dwarf variety that has grown up in the ground, or a natural seedling. Trees grown by grafting or layering may also be used. However, if a grafted tree is used, take care to choose one in which the joint is perfectly healed, or it will be impossible to grow a good bonsai from it. In the case of obtaining a tree by layering, remember that it takes two to three years before the roots develop.

Care

Fertilizer application is the same as with Kuro-Matsu (Japanese Black Pine), except that more fertilizer is needed. Once the roots have developed after transplanting or—in those years when the tree has not been transplanted—after the new buds have begun to grow, deposit two or three teaspoonfuls of fertilizer on the soil of the container about 5 or 6 times a year.

Nipping and removing old leaves

This, too, should be done as in the case of Kuro-Matsu (Japanese Black Pine). However, as the new buds of Goyō-Matsu (Five-Needled Pine) are shorter, only nip the tips of the buds.

Maintenance and pest control

Old leaves that have turned yellow should be removed by hand, but take care not to injure the bark. Red spiders, aphids, wooly aphids, and scales are common pests, so keep appropriate insecticides on hand.

Pruning the branches

Prune all unnecessary branches either when the old leaves are removed or in spring before the buds come out. This will help to shape the tree. Don't forget to smooth over the places where the branches have been pruned and, when the wound is large, take appropriate measures to prevent decay.

Arranging by wiring

At the time of the year when the sap is flowing vigorously, the branches are resilient but the least wound will cause the secretion of resin, which interferes with growth. Accordingly, with this type of tree, winter is the best time to arrange by wiring. In most cases you can use bare wire, but if you plan to bend the trunk or a thick branch use plenty of raffia. Change the wires every two years.

Carving

If carving is necessary on the trunk or branches, do this immediately before wiring. After wiring, let the tree rest so that it can recover its vitality.

Transplanting

Transplanting should be done in spring when the weather is warm. If you transplant too often, the leaves of your tree will tend to grow longer than is ideal. It is best just to transplant once every four or five years. Of course, if your tree develops root decay, or its branches begin to wither, you must transplant immediately, regardless of when it was last transplanted. Use red clay and coarse sand to plant your Goyō-Matsu, mixed in the proportion of 7:3 respectively.

Aka-Ezo-Matsu (Saghalien Spruce)

Characteristics

Since this tree has only a short history as bonsai, it is not yet known how long it will survive in a container. However, it is a very hardy plant which resists cold, snow, dryness and poor soil. Seeing how it flourishes in a container, developing fine branches and leaves, it is safe to assume that its lifespan is at least as long as that of Kuro-Matsu (Japanese Black Pine) or Goyō-Matsu (Five-Needled Pine).

This plant is indigenous to cold climates. Accordingly, its growth is slow but its bark is rough and has an elegance all of its own. Its leaves are much smaller and denser than those of Goyō-Matsu (Five-Needled Pine), and do not fall for several years. In spring, the beauty of its buds is remarkable. It is well suited to growing as a bonsai as it can be made to take almost any desired shape. And, once the tree has been given a certain shape, it will retain it for several years. Like Goyō-Matsu (Five-Needled Pine), its value as a bonsai will increase proportionately to the care it is given.

Varieties

The so-called Ezo-Matsu, is correctly called Aka-Ezo-Matsu by bonsai growers. It has thick, short, rounded leaves which grow densely and are yellowish-green in color. Its buds are particularly beautiful, and its trunk is a yellowish-brown. It grows very slowly. In contrast, the standard Ezo-Matsu or Kuro-Ezo-Matsu (Yesso Spruce) has leaves that are flat, long and narrow, and dark green in color. The trunk grows quite quickly, and is greyish-black in color. However, its leaves do not grow as densely as those of Aka-Ezo-Matsu, and its buds are not as beautiful, which explains why this variety is rarely grown as bonsai.

For use as bonsai, the Saghalien Spruce is the more suitable variety. If you are lucky you may stumble across a variety of Saghalien Spruce called the Eight Cluster Saghalien Spruce. The leaves of this variety are particularly short and dense, and the branches ramify into numerous smaller branches. This beautiful plant has a dwarfed form, and it does not take long to create a bonsai from a sapling. The Eight Cluster Saghalien Spruce is particularly suited for growing as a miniature bonsai, and is considered to be the king of the Yesso Spruce family!

Type of tree to use as bonsai

Needless to say, the best tree is one which has survived the harsh forces of nature out in the arctic tundra for 200 to 300 years. However, for practical purposes, any type that would grow to exhibit the characteristics of a large tree growing in the wild in a relatively short period of time is recommended.

If a suitable tree can be found you can obtain a tree to use as bonsai by layering. Choose a part where the branches are shapely and, when the buds come out, peel off the bark round the branch to a width of about 3 cm (1¼ inches) where you intend to layer the branch. Then smear some red clay mixed with water onto the place from which the bark has been peeled. Apply some wet sphagnum moss in a lump above the cut. Cover the moss with thin polyethylene film and fasten it with thread. See that the moss does not dry out. After the roots have developed sufficiently, the tree should be cut from the mother plant. If layering is used, one can easily obtain a tree in half a year from a mother plant that is 9 cm (3½ inches) in diameter.

It is also easy to grow a Saghalien Spruce or an Eight-Cluster Saghalien Spruce from a cutting. Spring is the best time to take cuttings. To begin with, find a small branch that is about two to three years old. It should be 9 to 15 cm (3½ to 6 inches) in length. Cut it off and plant it either in a flat box or a shallow pot, just like any other cutting. Water it frequently to encourage growth. Within half a year, you will have grown a tree that can be used for practicing the art of bonsai.

Once you have your potential bonsai, by whatever means, plant it firmly in a container with good water-drainage, filled with red clay and coarse sand mixed in a proportion of 8 : 2 respectively. Then place your tree where it will be sheltered from wind and strong sunlight. Syringe its leaves frequently to help its roots develop.

Care
The best place for this kind of tree is that same as that for Kuro-Matsu (Japanese Black Pine). In midsummer however, move it to a cool place. The plant should be placed where it will receive sunlight throughout the year. After planting it will take about a month for the roots to grow, and during this time you need to ensure that both the roots and the leaves get plenty of water. After that, up until summer, only water your tree at the roots, and that in small quantities. This will prevent the leaves from growing weak.

Throughout summer, water both the roots and the leaves to prevent the leaves from scorching and the branches from withering. Take care not to let the branches, leaves or trunk get too dry. At all other times ordinary watering should be sufficient.

Fertilizer application is the same as in the case of Goyō-Matsu (Five-Needled Pine), although the growth of young trees will be stimulated if fish manure is mixed with the rapeseed cake.

Nipping
Only nip those shoots that occur where you don't want dense thickets of branches or leaves growing. Start by nipping those that are growing the fastest. The length of time to continue nipping the shoots depends on the number of small branches the tree has and on the age of the tree, but in the case of a tree that already has a definite shape, about two weeks should be enough, provided nipping is done every two or three days.

Arranging the branches by wiring
New twigs should be arranged by wiring when their leaves have become hard; branches and trunks should be wired in winter. Bare wires may be used, unless you are bending old branches or trunks at acute angles, in which case it is best to wrap raffia around the places to be bent. If there are no twists in the wires, they need not be removed, but in general

Aka-Ezo-Matsu (Saghalien Spruce).
San-kan (Three trunks style).

they should be removed every two or three years and replaced by new wires, as wires tend to bite into the bark and harm it. Unnecessary branches—those which have grown contrary to the desired shape—should be cut off at the time the wires are applied.

Pest control

This plant has two great enemies: borers that attack the new buds, and red spiders that infect the tips of the new buds. To eradicate these, spray BHC (Benzene hexachloride) for the former and TEPP (Tetraethyll pyrophosphate) for the latter, just before the new buds come out.

Transplanting

Transplant every two years in the case of trees that are still growing, and every four to five years in the case of trees that have attained their permanent shape. Transplant in the spring when the buds begin to come out, using the same soil proportions as for Goyō-Matsu (Five-Needled Pine). Before transplanting, prune the roots. Young trees should have their roots pruned more closely than older trees. Transplant firmly into a container with good water drainage.

Carving

This is the same as for Goyō-Matsu (Five-Needled Pine).

Sugi (Japanese Cedar)

Characteristics

This is a hardy, rapid-growing tree. It has been adapted to growing in a container, and can survive in one for a long time. Its trunk is strong and straight, and the tree is particularly remarkable for the way it rises out of the ground. The branches ramify into numerous small branches, and the leaves are dwarfed in nature and dense. Despite being an evergreen, its leaves change color with the seasons. It is suited for growing as bonsai, especially in the Chokkan style, which has a single straight trunk. A tree which has been grown carefully in a container can capture the appearance of an old tree towering in the mist, deep in the mountains. Such a tree also reminds one of a solitary tree that stands in a field: a noble sentinel. It has a salient beauty of its own.

Varieties

There are numerous varieties of Sugi. Of these, the best one to grow as a bonsai is Ma-Sugi (True

Japanese Cedar). But there are also various kinds of Ma-Sugi, each with different bark, leaves, and such. Accordingly, take care to choose one with small, densely growing leaves and thick coarse bark.

Type of tree to use as bonsai

If one is fortunate enough to find a tree in the mountains with good leaves and bark, firmly developed roots, outspread branches, and a nice straight trunk, uproot it in spring just before budding time. In the ideal tree, however, the trunk should not be too thick or the tree will be too tall, and it will be hard to cut the trunk properly. So find a tree that has a trunk no more than 3 to 6 cm (1¼ to 2½ inches) in diameter, and that is between 45 and 61 cm/18 and 24½ inches tall. Any growth beyond this height should be cut off. The cut part should be made smooth and pointed.

As Sugi can be obtained easily by layering, trees that have been grown this way are perfectly suitable for growing as bonsai. The layering method is the same as that used to grow Aka-Ezo-Matsu (Saghalien Spruce).

The above measures are relevant if you are wanting to grow an average-sized bonsai. If, however, you

Sugi (Japanese Cedar)

92

want to grow a small bonsai, a seedling or a cutting is generally used. The former will be slow to grow taking at least 7 to 8 years before the tree has taken on a definite shape. The latter will grow more quickly, giving you a bonsai that is ready for viewing after only 4 or 5 years. But in terms of value as a bonsai, the latter is no match for the former.

Care

The tree must be planted firmly, but not too deep, in a container with good drainage. To help with drainage, put coarse sand at the bottom of the container. Place the container where it will get plenty of fresh air and sunlight. In summer, however, take care not to leave the container in direct sunlight, particularly in the afternoon, as this plant is vulnerable to hot weather. In winter, either put it indoors in a spot that gets plenty of light or in a cold-proof shelter to protect it from frost.

Make sure that the soil in the container is always a bit damp. Give it plenty of water in the summer, watering every morning and evening. In the winter, however, water it only in the mornings. If watering is done in the evening as well, there is the possibility that water will remain at the bottom of the container till night-time and freeze, thus harming the roots. Apply a weak liquid fertilizer, ideally, liquid compost, about twice a month during the growing season. In the fall, mix a bit of bone meal (in Japan, dried squid is recommended) into the fertilizer and give it plenty of water, as this plant usually needs more water than other species.

Nipping

The beauty of your Sugi will be greatly enhanced if you encourage the leaves to grow fine, dense tips. To do this, the buds need to be nipped several times throughout the growing season. Do this by hand rather than with shears, when the new buds have grown to a length of about 15 mm (½ inch).

Maintenance and arranging by wiring

In early spring, just before budding time, cut off all the branches that have withered or become too dense. You should also prune overgrown branches to maintain the shape of your tree. This is also the time to arrange unsightly branches and branches that interfere with the desired shape of your tree by wiring. However, in the case of growing a Chokkan style bonsai (a bonsai which has a single straight-trunk), wiring should be no more than a mere aid.

Transplanting

A tree that is still growing should be transplanted every two years. All other types of tree should be transplanted every three to four years, early in the spring. The soil should be 5 parts black loam, 3 parts coarse sand, and 2 leaf mold.

Carving and the top 'jin'

Sugi often feature a *jin* (weathered dead top). If you choose to make such a feature on your tree, do not forget to attach wires to another healthy branch nearby in order to raise the next growth point.

It is possible to see a *jin* growing naturally from a tree that is growing in the wild under severe conditions. There are *jin* whose branches are dead. These are called *ten-jin* (top *jin*). Also, there are *jin* which grow out of rocks. There are jin which are made out of thick branches which have withered away. The bark of these branches has been peeled off and bleached naturally into a bone-white hue. Also, in the case of *shari-kan* the bark or woody part of the trunk has been completely carved out.

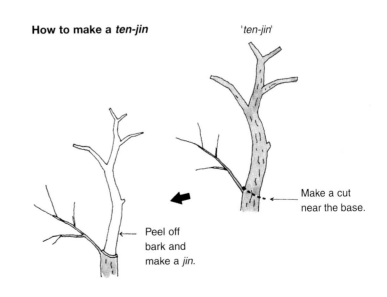

How to make a *ten-jin*

'ten-jin'

Peel off bark and make a *jin*.

Make a cut near the base.

Deciduous Flowering Trees

Ume (Flowering Japanese Apricot)

Characteristics

This is a particularly hardy, rapid-growing tree. It withstands the cold very well, and bears beautiful flowers early in the spring, long before all the other trees bloom. It has a refreshing fragrance, too. The trunk has a sensual curve, and the bark is very strong and coarse. The way it stretches its branches has an air of primitive grace. The tree increases in dignity as it grows older. Both its shape and its flowers offer perpetual enjoyment to all who view the plant. It is suitable to grow as bonsai, as it can be made to take almost any shape. Moreover, it is easy to grow, has a long life-span and, with good care, its value as bonsai can be considerable. When in bloom, this tree is indeed the king of bonsai.

Varieties

At one time, there were over 300 varieties, but today the number stands at about half this. And of these, only about one-third or 50 varieties are suitable for bonsai. These 50 varieties are roughly classified into two groups according to the color of the blossoms: white and red. Both varieties have single and double petals. They can also be classified according to whether the flowers are large, medium, or small. The best kind, however, is the fragrant, single-petaled variety that has medium to large flowers.

The drooping branches of this variety, found both among white and red Flowering Japanese Apricots, have a particular grace. They are called Shidare-Ume (Drooping Japanese Apricot). This variety is highly prized by some bonsai lovers.

Type of tree to use as bonsai

Formerly, an old tree uprooted from the mountains was sought to use as bonsai. Today, however, such trees are no longer available. Instead, specimens are acquired either by grafting onto a two-year old seedling, or by growing from a cutting. Whichever kind you have, trim the branches and roots close and plant the tree in the garden in early spring (around February), after its blossoms have fallen. Give it plenty of fertilizer so that it will develop fine roots

and branches. In autumn, dig it up again after it has shed its leaves, trim its branches and roots closely again, replant it and give it more fertilizer. By repeating this process over a period of two to three years, the trunk should become thick and the general shape of the tree will be quite strongly defined. By now the tree will be old enough to start flowering, so this is also the time to plant your tree in its container.

Care

The best soil for this type of tree is a mixture of black loam, Kanuma soil, and coarse sand in the proportions 6:2:2 respectively. An azalea-pot or a container made from shallow unglazed pottery is most suitable. The best time to plant your tree in its container is just after the flowering season. Before planting, carefully examine the shape of your tree, then cut off all unnecessary branches, leaving two or three one-year-old branches. Next, trim the fine roots short and then plant in a container with good drainage.

The container must be placed where there is plenty of sunlight and air.

Water the plant whenever the surface of the soil in the container becomes dry. Give it plenty of water, especially during budding time and in summer. Do not apply fertilizer until about three weeks after moving the plant to its container. When using liquid fertilizer, apply it two or three times a month; in the case of solid fertilizer, deposit it on the surface of the soil about once a month. Continue using fertilizer until the end of the hot season.

Until early summer, only use rapeseed cake as fertilizer. This should be made into a weak liquid fertilizer and applied several times. Later, fertilizer of an animal nature, for instance, bone meal obtained from fish or chicken droppings, should be applied, mixed with a small amount of superphosphate. This fertilizer should be somewhat stronger to encourage the plant to blossom profusely.

Nipping

New buds that are growing too close together and unwanted shoots that may otherwise grow weak and long should be nipped at the base as soon as they appear. For those shoots which are left, only nip the tips of those that tend to grow too long. Nip at about the time when the leaves have lost their softness. Take great care when nipping the buds. If new buds are nipped indiscriminately, there is a danger that the branches will not grow thick, and they may even wither in winter. There is also a risk of reducing the

Shidare-Ume
(Flowering Japanese
Apricot with drooping
branches)

Ume (Flowering Japanese Apricot)
Miniature Bonsai

amount of blossom to only a few flowers. New buds should be left to grow till the summer and then nipped from the branches.

Arranging the branches by wiring

The time that you nip the buds of your tree is also the time to arrange the branches by wiring. This should be done using paper-wrapped wires. However, this is not always necessary. In fact, in the case of old branches or trunks, it is better to arrange the branches of your tree by suspension.

Pest control

Common pests are stem borers, caterpillars, aphids and scales. These can best be eradicated by spraying suitable insecticides at the time of their outbreak.

Maintenance and pruning the branches

The best time to prune the branches is in the spring after the new buds have appeared. After studying the overall appearance of the tree, cut off all unnecessary branches. Then, by looking at the condition of the buds and assessing whether they look weak or strong, prune the branches which have developed in the previous year to a proper length.

Carving

During winter, carve off any decayed areas from trunks and thick branches. These areas should be carved completely smooth, then covered by adhesive plaster or wax-cloth.

Protection from cold in winter

Although Ume is a tree that generally withstands the cold well, sometimes winter cold can wither the branches and injure the leaves. So, in winter, after the plant has been exposed to two or three light frosts, either put it inside where it will get plenty of light, or in a frost-proof shelter. If the plant is watered during this period and the temperature is maintained at 60–70°F (15–20°C), the early blossoming varieties will begin to grow flowers after about a month.

Points to bear in mind during blossom time The tree should be given plenty of sunlight, water and air. Before the flowers open, the tree should be sprinkled with water as often as possible. If there are too many flower-buds, they should be thinned out. Those flowers which have faded should be nipped off so that they will not develop into fruit.

Transplanting

Ume should be transplanted once a year, after the blossoming season is over. At this time prune all the branches except the one-year old branches that you are growing so that there will be more flowers in the next season. Plants that may be treated in the same manner as Ume, are Sanzashi (Japanese Hawthorn), and Kaidō (Showy Crab Apple).

Boke (Flowering Japanese Quince)

Characteristics

Unlike large trees such as pines and Ume (Flowering Japanese Apricot), Boke is a bush that develops branches and leaves close to the ground. This makes it more suitable for growing in clusters, as it grows in nature, than for growing as a solitary bonsai. Boke is a hardy tree that has a lifespan of over a hundred years. Buds appear very vigorously, so can be nipped without fear of overdoing it. It puts forth numerous branches that have a primitive elegance. Its flowers, which begin to bloom in winter and continue into spring, are varicolored. Some varieties have large fruit, the appearance of which enhances the beauty of the tree considerably. It is suitable for growing as a bonsai. It is also an easy tree to grow, so all bonsai-growers should try to have at least one Boke.

Varieties

There are various varieties of Boke, but the kinds most commonly used as bonsai are the following:
(1) Kusa-Boke. Less than one meter high, with thin branches and thorns. Its flowers are single-petaled, and range from crimson to white in color. It bears a lot of fruit.
(2) Choju-bai. A dwarf variety of Boke. There are two kinds, those that bear red flowers and those that bear white. The tree has flowers almost all the year round.
(3) Kan-Boke. This blooms very early in the year. The most common variety has single-petaled red flowers, but other varieties have flowers that are white, red with white stripes, and red with light brown stripes.
(4) Boke that blooms in spring. There are numerous kinds. They all have thick branches which are not too dense, and the single-petaled flowers are large and brilliantly colored.

Type of tree to use as bonsai

In the case of Kusa-Boke, a wild tree or one that has grown in the ground rather than in a pot is the most

Kan-Boke (Flowering
Japanese Quince)

Kan-Boke (Flowering Japanese
Quince)
Miniature Bonsai

suitable for bonsai, while in the case of Choju-bai, grafted trees are used. As for Kan-Boke and Boke that blooms in spring, plants propagated by division or cuttings may be used. In both cases, remember that all Boke are susceptible to nematode worms and parasites that cause warts to develop near the roots, so when you choose your tree be sure to check that it is disease free.

Care

The soil in the container should be a mix of black loam and red clay, and approximately one third coarse sand. The best time to plant your tree in its container is autumn, after its leaves have fallen. However, as long as you plant while the buds are still hard, early spring is just as good. As for where to place your Boke, the same rules apply as for Ume (Flowering Japanese Apricot). But in mid-summer, the direct sunlight in the afternoon should be avoided. Watering should be the same as in the case of any other plant. The leaves only need additional watering immediately after transplanting, during budding-time and when the buds begin to open. Fertilizer application is the same as for Ume (Japanese Flowering Apricot).

Summer pruning

During the growing stage new buds will sprout all the time. Check for buds which are growing unevenly and prune them as soon as they appear. Those that have been left should be allowed to grow thick and long. When the new twigs have become more or less hard, trim off all but a few leaves. This will make the secondary buds sprout vigorously. The secondary shoots should also be allowed to grow long and thick.

Trimming the branches

Allow the secondary branches, that is, those which have developed from secondary buds, to grow thick until autumn. Then, after the leaves have fallen, trim them to suitable lengths, leaving only one to two buds on each branch. At the same time, trim all branches that have lost their vitality, have grown too dense, or have withered, to protect the general shape of the tree. Wiring should be done only when unavoidable. Usually, it should be possible to arrange the branches just by trimming.

Transplanting

Transplanting should be done once a year in autumn after the leaves have fallen.

Fuji (Japanese Wisteria)

Characteristics

As Fuji is a climbing plant, it may seem a strange choice to grow as bonsai. It can, however, be used for bonsai by cutting the tendrils short. It has many attractive features of its own—a thick and graceful trunk with numerous bends, thick, short branches that grow sparsely from the trunk, and long trailing garlands of flowers that show themselves from underneath the verdure of its young leaves. It flowers in late spring, is comparatively easy to grow, and is extremely long-lived.

Varieties

There are more than twenty varieties, and their flowers range in color from purple to white. The flowers may be single or double-petaled. The length of the flower garlands is usually about 30 cm (12 inches), but some grow up to one meter. Of these varieties, the one most commonly used for bonsai is Yama-Fuji which has a thick coarse bark. Its flowers are white or purple, single-petaled, and large. The garlands are not particularly long, ranging from 15 to 20 cm (6 to 8 inches).

Type of tree to use as bonsai

If a mother tree is obtained from the mountains or fields, its roots will not develop very easily. On the other hand, seedlings from seeds take about twenty years before they bear any blossoms. So the most common choice is a grafted tree, which will bear flowers in a relatively short time. The problem even with grafted trees is that if they are transplanted into a container, they will take a long time to bear flowers. The solution, therefore, is to use young trees that are four to five years old and have flower-buds.

When purchasing a grafted tree, note the following points:
(1) The grafting should be done as close to the roots of the stock as possible. The joint should be thoroughly healed so that it is inconspicuous.
(2) The tree must be healthy, and free of all diseases, including nematodes at the root.
(3) The tree should not be too tall, and should have numerous branches in its lower parts.
(4) It should be a well-known variety and should have many flower-buds.

The best time to purchase a plant is in autumn after the leaves have fallen.

Care

In the case of a grafted tree, prune its tendrils and roots short enough so that it can be planted in the container. Plant it temporarily in the ground to develop its root system. After about a month, the tree will have numerous white roots. At a suitable time, dig up the plant, being careful not to hurt the roots, then plant it in a container filled with equal parts of black loam and red clay. Water drainage must be satisfactory.

After planting, give the tree plenty of water and put it in a cold-proof shelter. Water the tree and roots once every day to ensure good root growth. With the coming of the warm spring in the following year, put the plant outdoors. Apply weak liquid fertilizer made from rapeseed cake at the end of the flowering season, alternating it with solid fertilizer deposited on the surface of the soil. When the new vines have developed and the leaves have hardened, apply fertilizer twice a month during the flowering season from April to May. This fertilizer should be deposited on the soil surface and should consist of rapeseed cake, mixed with bone meal and a small amount of superphosphate. In June, after the flowering season is over, prune the branches, leaving only a few, and cut the tips off these. The branches should be pruned from the base. In autumn give the plant stronger liquid rapeseed fertilizer, then deposit some fertilizer on the soil surface. Both types of fertilizer should be given at least once, and after that, no more fertilizer. It is said that Fuji requires from three to four times as much fertilizer as most bonsai, since its trunk tends to be more energetic than that of other trees. For this reason, care should be taken to give it plenty of water and fertilizer, as lack of water can be particularly harmful to its flowers.

Water just enough to keep the soil surface thoroughly moist. In midsummer, a plant which so far has been watered two to three times a day should be watered only once in two days. This will cause the tips of the vines and leaves to look withered during the daytime. When this happens, place the container in water and let it absorb all the water it needs. Repeat this process two or three times at intervals of five to six days. The result will be that the vines will stop growing and the buds will become flower-buds. This is how grafted wisteria trees can be made to bear flowers.

Arranging the branches

By nature, Fuji grows by clinging to other objects. Its branches are sparse, its leaves large, and its flowers hang down in garlands. Due to its particular charac-teristics, it is best grown as a cascading or semi-cascading bonsai.

In this style of bonsai, the trunk grows obliquely or bends to one side. To obtain the most appropriate shape, the branches must be distributed evenly on both the left and right sides of the trunk. The resilient branches of Fuji are particularly well suited to this kind of arrangement. The trunk and branches should be arranged by wiring or suspended in spring when the new buds begin to appear. In the case of new vines, apply paper-wrapped wire after the leaves have more or less hardened. As the vines of Fuji have a tendency to entwine themselves clockwise, any wires that are applied should be wound in the same direction, and the branches must be bent while twisting them in the same direction.

Trimming the new vines

When Fuji is grown in a container, the vines naturally tend to become shorter. However, if the plant is young, the vines should still show great vitality despite being in a container. Trimming the vines indiscriminately will jeopardize the growth of your bonsai and stop it from bearing flower-buds. To prevent this, allow the vines to grow until the leaves have more or less hardened, then nip or bend the tips of the vines. Then, after the leaves have fallen in autumn, leave one to three vines, and trim the rest.

All unnecessary branches should be cut off immediately after the flowering season.

Clipping the beans

After flowering, Fuji bears legume-like fruit. The sight of these legumes hanging from the tree has a peculiar beauty of its own, but if too many of them are allowed to grow, they weaken the plant. So just leave a few and cut off the rest as soon as possible.

Transplanting

Transplant every year immediately after the flowering season. At this time, also cut off any withered or aged roots leaving only the vigorous roots. These roots should be bundled up and the tree planted in the container again.

Deciduous Trees with Autumnal Tints

Momiji (Japanese Maple)

Characteristics

This hardy tree can withstand extremes of heat and cold. It can endure trimming quite well and has a long lifespan in a container. Its trunk tends to develop firm roots and rises gracefully from the ground. The trunk and the bark have an elegance all of their own. Its dense branches have delicate tips, giving the tree a soft and graceful appearance. The shape of the leaves resembles a hand, and they are edged with points like the teeth of a saw. The tree is beautiful to look at in spring when the buds come out, in summer when the leaves are green, but most of all the tree is an object of surpassing beauty when the leaves have turned scarlet. The tree is also extremely beautiful after the leaves have fallen, for it reminds one of a winter landscape in nature.

The tree is particularly suitable for growing as bonsai as it can be made to take almost any desired shape. The process of growing, too, is very simple, and any care bestowed on the plant will be richly repaid by increasing its value as a bonsai. Ranking only next to the pine-tree and Ume (Flowering Japanese Apricot), Momiji is one of the most important bonsai plants.

Varieties

There are many varieties, but for bonsai, varieties with small, dense leaves are preferred. For example, Yama-Momiji and Seigen.

Points to bear in mind when growing bonsai

Although Momiji can still be found in the mountains, seedlings, grafted trees, and trees obtained by layering may also be used. There are various ways to grow these plants as bonsai and to arrange their shape, but the most important thing to remember when growing Momiji is to create a shape that is both graceful and delicate. The trunk must be round, straight, and without scars, and the branches must be arranged gracefully and delicately, with an almost feminine beauty.

The best way to grow a plant like this is to start with a seedling. In the following pages we will explain the best way for a beginner to grow a bonsai from a seedling. This technique is also the most up-to-date.

How to plant the seeds

Use fully ripe seeds from a Yama-Momiji (Wild Maple) which has small, dense leaves and is beautiful when its leaves change color in autumn. Dry the seeds in the shade and immerse them inwater. Select those which sink to the bottom, and plant them immediately.

The best place to plant the seeds is in a flat, shallow container. Put a layer of coarse sand at the bottom of the container, then put in lumps of red clay about the size of millet grains. After this, fill about one-third of the container with small irregularly-shaped pebbles that will lie stably in the container. Instead of pebbles, one may also use clayey soil, kneaded into cone-shaped lumps.

Scatter the seeds in a thin layer on top of the pebbles or lumps of clay. Then add enough earth to cover the seeds. Water them gently with a sprinkler and place the container in the shade.

Growing a young tree

Watering is necessary only if there is a danger that the soil might dry out. Generally, dew and rain should be sufficient. The seeds will sprout the next spring. The young plants should be put outdoors when two or three leaves have opened, in a place that will get the morning but not the afternoon sun. Water whenever the soil gets dry.

Apply weak liquid fertilizer from time to time. Thin out overcrowded plants so that the leaves do not overlap. On hot summer days, put the container in semi-shade where there is a good breeze. When the time comes for the leaves to fall, the plants will be about 10 to 20 cm (4 to 8 inches) tall. In winter, either place the container indoors or bury the container in theground to protect it against frost and cold. Do not neglect watering during this period. Make sure that the soil in the container does not dry out. When the weather becomes warm again in spring, place the container on a shelf so that the plant will be exposed to sunshine all day. Fertilizer should be applied once in May, but only to bonsai which have not been transplanted. Do not put fertilizer on bonsai which were transplanted in the spring.

How to arrange the leaves

In the second year, the terminal bud will first appear, followed by the appearance of lateral buds in the

Illustration showing how Momiji (Japanese Maple) and Tō-Kaede (Trident Maple) are planted on rocks

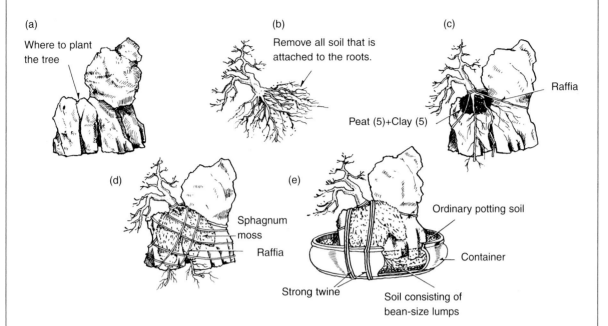

(a) Where to plant the tree

(b) Remove all soil that is attached to the roots.

(c) Raffia
Peat (5)+Clay (5)

(d) Sphagnum moss
Raffia

(e) Ordinary potting soil
Container
Strong twine
Soil consisting of bean-size lumps

The purpose of a bonsai on a rock is to reproduce the natural appearance of a tree perched on a rocky outcrop. The best time for planting this type of bonsai is in spring just before the buds sprout. Momiji (Japanese Maple) and Tō-Kaede (Trident Maple) are both suitable for this type of bonsai, and the same method may be used for either tree. Beginners are urged to try with either plant.

Explanation of the Illustration.

(a) Rock for use in planting a bonsai on a rock. The rock must be attractively shaped, neither too large nor too small, and must be stable. It must have a dent, groove or crack in it in which the tree can be planted. A rock of a dark and subdued color should be chosen.

(b) Tree for use in planting a bonsai on a rock. Whether you choose a Momiji (Japanese Maple) or a Tō-Kaede (Trident Maple), be sure that it is a young tree with a more or less definite shape. Its lower branches must be thick and hang down, and its roots must be fine, numerous and long.

(c) How to plant the tree. Remove all soil adhering to the roots. Make up a mixture that is equal parts of peat and clay kneaded with water, then apply a thick coating to the dent in the rock. Place the tree on this mixture, then divide the roots into three or four bunches, and position the tree so that it stands on the rock as gracefully as possible. Use raffia to tie the base of the trunk firmly to the rock.

(d) Distribution of the roots. Distribute the main roots, one by one, down the cracks or grooves in the rock, toward its base. Smear the mixture of peat and clay on the rock so that the roots will cling firmly. After all the main roots have been attached to the rock, follow the same procedure to secure the smaller roots to the rock. Lastly cover the roots with a thin coating of sphagnum moss. Tie everything down with raffia.

(e) After planting the tree on the rock, choose a shallow container that is somewhat larger than the rock, and plant the tree in the container, rock and all. Plant the tree as shown in the illustration. Any roots with tips that could not be fastened to the rock should be buried in the container, taking care not to hurt them and at the same time making sure that the root ends are planted in a graceful manner. After the tree and rock have been placed in the container, use twine to fasten the rock securely to the container. Water well. After this, treat the plant as you would any other tree that has been recently transplanted.

nodes in the upper part of the tree. The leaves on Momiji grow in pairs, one on each side of the branch. So, the lateral buds, like the leaves, also grow in pairs.

When the young shoots become about 20 cm (8 inches) long, the top of the terminal bud should be nipped to prevent the tree from growing any further and to stimulate the development of the lateral buds. If you allow the lateral buds to grow in pairs, the tree will become unsightly. For this reason they should be nipped so that they grow alternately, one on the left side, then the next one on the right, and so on. All unnecessary lateral buds should be nipped as soon as possible, so that the basic form of the tree gradually takes shape.

This method is used for bonsai that have been planted together in a group. In this situation take care not to arrange the branches of the young trees too uniformly or the result will be monotonous. Your aim should be to arrange the trees in such a way that the whole creates an illusion of a cluster of Momiji growing on a rock or hill. Discard any unwanted seedlings, and correct those that have an unattractive shape by wiring.

Saplings growing on the outside of the cluster should have their inside branches pruned and their outside branches left. The seedlings in the middle should have their lower branches thinned, and their thick branches made to grow alternately to the left and to the right, while their small branches should be made to grow forward and backward. In other words, the branches should be pruned so that no two branches are located exactly opposite each other.

Care

Place your trees where they will get plenty of sunlight, fresh air, and a breeze. In summer, put them where they will get three or four hours of morning sun, then move them to a spot that is shady and cool for the rest of the day. In winter, they should be placed in a cold-proof shelter or in a room to protect them from the cold. They should be watered as for all other plants. Beside normal watering in spring when the buds appear, syringe them once a day; in summer, water once in the morning and once in the evening.

While the seedlings are growing, use both liquid and composite fertilizer, always taking into consideration the color of the leaves and the general condition of the plants. Eradicate any insects that infest the leaves or branches.

Bud-nipping

Cut off the terminal bud once your tree has attained a height of about 10 cm (4 inches), leaving about two nodes. Leave some lateral buds for thickening, but prune the others, when they have grown about three nodes, down to the first node. When the secondary buds appear, leave just one that is in good condition. Let this shoot grow till it is about two nodes long, then cut it off after the first node. Nipping the new buds in this manner, before they become too thick, is the secret of making a delicately shaped tree that has no scars.

Arranging the branches by wiring

Do this when the leaves have more or less hardened, using wire wrapped with paper to protect the soft bark that is characteristic of Momiji. The softness of the bark makes it possible to arrange even four or five-year-old trunks or branches.

Leaf-cutting

The purpose of leaf-cutting is to make the leaves of Yama-Momiji even smaller and denser, and to make their tips more delicate, softer and closer. The technique of leaf-cutting has been explained above.

Transplanting

If Momiji is transplanted every year, it will overstimulate the growth of the plant, causing the tree to lose its shape. In addition, the branches will become rough, and the leaves large and sparse. Therefore, only transplant once every three or four years. When transplanting Momiji, be sure to remove it from the container without taking it apart from the rock or the block of peat (see illustration). Next, remove some of the soil from the roots, prune the tips of the roots and all unnecessary branches, and then plant it again in a flat container. The soil in the container should have a mixture of five parts black loam, three red clay, and two coarse sand. It is also important to have a layer of coarse sand at the bottom of the pot to ensure good drainage.

If the method described here is followed, the tree will become a fairly presentable bonsai in about three years. After about ten years, the thick roots will twine together, the trunks and branches will gain an appearance of age, and the bonsai will give the viewer more joy than any single tree can give. Other trees that may be treated in the same manner as Momiji are Tō-Kaede (Trident Maple), and Soro, (Loose-Flowered Hornbeam).

Kaede (Japanese Maple) planted on the rock.

Deciduous Trees that Bear Fruit

Ume-modoki (*Ilex serrata* var. Sieboldii)

Characteristics

From late autumn until late winter, this plant is decked with countless coral-red berries about the size of soy beans. Of the many fruit-bearing plants that are used as bonsai, this is an outstanding plant that has always enjoyed unsurpassed popularity.

Varieties

There are many varieties of Ume-modoki beside the one described above. One bears white berries, and a third bears berries of both pink and white. Both of these are used as bonsai, but the ordinary kind that bears red berries easily surpasses all other varieties in popularity.

Type of tree to use as bonsai

Either a wild tree from the mountains or one that grows in the garden may be used, provided it has the makings of a bonsai and shapely branches. In most cases, however, one starts with a seedling. The former often have wart-like swellings where the trunk or branches have been cut, while the latter have the disadvantage that the grower has to wait ten or more years before the plant bears berries.

For beginners, it is better not to go to a great deal of trouble finding a suitable tree and growing it from scratch, but to buy a bonsai which already bears berries and has a definite shape. It involves less expense, and one can start enjoying the tree from the very first day.

Care

Place the plant on an outdoor shelf that will be sheltered in winter from cold winds, frost and snow. Although it generally requires no more water than any other plant, it needs a lot of watering from the time its flowers begin to open until it puts out berries. If it doesn't have enough water at this time it may not produce berries.

During the growing season, give your plant weak liquid fertilizer once or twice a month. After the summer, it will not need as much fertilizer as do other fruit-bearing plants.

Nipping

Nip new buds that have begun to develop and unwanted buds as soon as possible. Allow the remaining buds to grow until about the time the leaves harden. Then, after taking the arrangement of the branches into consideration, nip these shoots to about 3 to 6 cm (1¼ to 2½ inches) in length. When

Ume-modoki (*Ilex serrata* var. Sieboldii)

Ume-modoki (Deciduous Holly; *Ilex serrata* var. Sieboldii)

the secondary buds appear, nip off those that are unnecessary and let the rest grow.

Arranging the shape of the tree by wiring

Once the leaves on the new shoots have hardened, cut off the tips of the shoots and arrange them using wire wrapped in paper. When doing this, bear in mind that Ume-modoki is a plant that snaps easily. To make it more workable, refrain from watering your plant for a day or two prior to wiring, and when you begin wiring do not bend any branches at acute angles. When you have finished wiring, give it plenty of water so that it can regain its vitality.

Transplanting

Transplant every spring just before the buds come out. At the same time, shape the tree by pruning the branches that were new the year before. If you cut off an old branch, be sure to carve smooth the place where the cut was made and apply wax cloth to it in the form of a cross. The best soil for transplanting is a mixture of 7 parts black loam to 3 parts red clay or Kanuma soil.

Picking the berries

The red berries of Ume-modoki become even redder if they are exposed once or twice to light frost. But then it is best to bring the plant indoors to enjoy its display of red berries. However, if the berries are allowed to stay on the tree too long, they exhaust the plant, with the result that there will be fewer berries the following year. Therefore, pick all the berries after about a month.

Shimpaku (Chinese Juniper)

Characteristics

This is a very hardy tree that can survive for hundreds of years in a container. When the trunk becomes very old, most of its bark falls off and the wood part decays, leaving only the core of the tree. Even under such adverse conditions, the tree manages to survive on the little remaining bark, giving an impression of venerable grandeur. The branches are fine and dense, and its leaves green, short and rope-shaped. The foliage which covers the tree is a source of enjoyment to the viewer, no less than the shapely trunk. The reason that Shimpaku is so highly prized as bonsai is that it always shows great vigor in spite of its age, and the tenacity with which it survives gives the tree a venerable appearance.

Varieties

There are many varieties related to Shimpaku. There is a variety with leaves like those of the Sugi (Japanese Cedar), and branches that creep close to the ground called Haibyaku-Shin (Creeping Japanese Juniper). There is another variety which is planted in gardens, called Kaizuka-Ibuki, a third variety with yellow variegated leaves called Ōgon Ibuki (*Juniperus chinensis* var. *aureo-globosa*), and a fourth variety that has an extremely dwarfed form and is used as a border for flower-beds, called Tama-Ibuki (*Juniperus chinensis* var. *globosa*). Of these varieties, however, only Shimpaku is suitable to grow as bonsai.

Type of tree to use as bonsai

The best tree to use would be a plant two or three hundred years old, found on some precipice in the deep mountains or an unexplored valley—a tree that has withstood the austerity of all weathers, and whose branches and trunk are bent or partially bleached.

However, such old trees are so hard to obtain. The usual custom therefore is to start with a cutting.

Of course, a tree like this cannot be compared with an old tree that has been uprooted from the mountains, but it can be made to take almost any shape. If you plant it on a rock and grow it in the cascade style of bonsai, it will develop into a beautiful bonsai after just a few years.

Care

Place your plant where there is plenty of sunlight and fresh air. At night, expose your plant to the night dew. Water the same as with any other plant but, in addition, syringe the leaves twice a day through the summer, once in the morning and once in the evening. In winter once a day is enough. When syringing, ensure that the water reaches both sides of the leaves as well as all the branches and the trunk.

Apply weak liquid fertilizer made from rapeseed cake once a week during both the budding season in spring and the growing season. Never, under any circumstances, give your tree strong fertilizer. Excessive fertilizer will cause the branches to grow too long and the tree to lose its shape.

Nipping

The new buds of Shimpaku are three-pronged and appear in spring and autumn. Nip the central bud before it hardens. A day or two later, nip the two buds that remain on either side. If you nip the buds

like this—as soon as they have appeared—secondary buds will appear after four or five days. They will appear at the base of the place from which the primary buds were removed.

These secondary buds, too, should be nipped in the same way. The secondary buds will be followed by tertiary buds. Thus, in the case of Shimpaku, it is necessary to repeat the process of nipping all through the budding season. This is the secret of increasing the number of branches and of making the bud-tips fine, dense and beautiful.

Trimming the branches

If the bud-tips of Shimpaku become too dense, the lower and middle branches will be impeded in their development, resulting in a top-heavy appearance. An overgrown tree is a very unsightly thing so, to avoid this, nip the branches at least once a year. The best time to trim is in spring before the buds come out. Prune any branches that point upward, those which are growing vigorously, and those which have grown too long. Also prune withered and dense branches. Butbefore pruning each branch, make sure that there is a small or young branch under the branch that you are about to cut off.

How to dispose of cedar-like leaves

It sometimes happens that Shimpaku develops cedar-like leaves—long, needle-type leaves. This is a very common phenomenon that occurs in trees that have lost their vitality, but which, upon applying fertilizer, regain their strength. These cedar-like leaves greatly reduce the value of Shimpaku as bonsai. If this happens, you must transplant the tree at a suitable time and give it proper fertilizer. Merely cutting

Shimpaku (Chinese Juniper) with a beautiful *shari-kan* trunk with weathered and worn bark). This was found in the wild and is 250 years old.

off such leaves will not cure the problem. If you wish to cut the leaves off, however, wait until the tree has sufficiently recovered its vitality.

How to prevent leaf-burn
In mid-summer, if the tree is exposed to very strong sunlight, and water is scarce, leaf-burn will take place. To prevent this, keep your plant out of the afternoon sun in midsummer, and give it plenty of water.

Transplanting
Transplant every three years in the spring when the buds begin to appear. Transplant into soil that is 7 parts red clay and 3 parts coarse sand. Also put a thin layer of crushed limestone at the bottom of the container.

Toshō (Needle Juniper)

Characteristics
This is a hardy tree that can survive a long time. It has a hard, straight trunk, and is suitable for growing Chokkan style bonsai, with a single straight trunk. Old trees with dense dark-green needles with short grooves or white stomas (pores) on their surface have an aspect of grandeur such as few other bonsai can boast. It can also be grown as a miniature bonsai. It is simple to grow.

Varieties
There are many varieties related to Toshō, such as Yore-Nezu (*Juniperus rigida* var. *filiformis* Maxim) with its leaves that twist in a spiral, Hai-Nezu (Shore Juniper) whose branches and trunk crawl along the ground, and Shidare-Nezu the tips of whose branches droop down. But none of these varieties can compare with Toshō as a tree to grow as bonsai.

Type of tree to use as bonsai
Usually, an old tree is uprooted from a crack in a rock in the mountains, or a young tree is uprooted in spring around budding time, and then grown in the garden for a year or two. Or, if you don't mind that the plant will be slow to put down roots, you can use a cutting or a tree obtained by layering.

Planting
The best soil for planting is a mixture of coarse sand and 30 to 40% red clay. The container should be of medium depth and made of unglazed pottery. Put a layer of gravel or lumpy earth at the bottom to

Toshō (Needle Juniper) Ne-tsuranari (Root-Connected Style)

ensure good drainage. In the case of an old tree, cut the trunk to a suitable height before planting. Since Tosho grow in the wild under severe conditions, its withered branches and trunk, with their bone white color, have the appearance of trees which have been swept by strong winds but have somehow survived. Its tip, therefore, should be made into a *jin* (top which is dead and weathered) by peeling off the bark and giving it a feeling of old age, thereby adding to the elegance of the bonsai.

107

Care

Syringe the leaves frequently until the roots have developed. Start giving fertilizer only after this. The best place for your plant is the same as that for Shimpaku. Syringing the leaves with water is the best way to water this tree; the best fertilizer is the same as that for Kuro-Matsu (Japanese Black Pine). Too much fertilizer will cause excessive growth of the branches and leaves.

Nipping

The technique of nipping is the same as for Sugi (Japanese Cedar). While the new buds continue to appear, nip with the fingers as often as necessary. Using shears for this will harm the tree.

Arranging by wiring

New twigs should be wired when the leaves have more or less hardened; for young trunks and branches the best time is in spring before buds appear. Use paper-wrapped wires for the new twigs. For other parts, wrap raffia around areas that are to be bent then apply bare wire. Cut off all unwanted branches and arrange the shape of the tree at the same time as wiring.

Carving

You will need to carve the tree to remove any decayed parts of the trunk if you want to make the top part of the trunk into a *jin*, or if you want to turn a branch into a *jin* by removing the bark. All carving should be done in winter.

Transplanting

Transplant every three or four years when the new buds begin to appear. The soil for planting is as explained above. Change the container for a permanent one when the tree has taken on a more or less definite shape. The permanent container is the one in which the bonsai will be admired after it reaches its final shape, and it is chosen because its shape and material suit the bonsai both for growing and for aesthetic purposes. Round containers made from mud are popular.

Keyaki (Zelkova)

Characteristics

Of the many types of deciduous tree, this is especially prized for the grandeur and delicate beauty of its appearance in winter. It is suitable for growing as bonsai, as it can be made to take almost any desired shape. It is most suited for growing as a solitary bonsai with a straight trunk. The technique for this is not difficult. Keyaki is a hardy tree that can survive many years in a container. It is beautiful to look at in spring when the buds come out, but even more so in autumn when the leavesassume their autumnal tints. Among the various kinds of deciduous tree used for bonsai, this species ranks with Momiji (Japanese Maple) and Tō-Kaede (Trident Maple), and is surpassed only by Ume (Flowering Japanese Apricot).

Varieties

There are two varieties of Keyaki—those that have a reddish tint when the new buds come out, and those that have a greenish tint. The former has smaller and denser leaves than the latter, and its autumnal tints are more beautiful. Both varieties show great variation, depending on individual trees, in the size of the leaves and coarseness of the bark. For a choice bonsai, select a tree with reddish buds, small leaves, and bark that is thick, rugged and strong.

Type of tree to use as bonsai

Use either a cutting or a tree obtained by layering. Or, if you can find one, you can uproot a tree from the mountains and fields. However, as Keyaki, like Momiji (Japanese Maple), is prized for its smooth round trunk rising vigorously from its firm roots, it is best to start with a seedling that is a year old. Such a specimen will also grow quickly, and should give you a good bonsai that can be enjoyed in 3 or 4 years.

Planting a seedling

Choose a healthy plant with reddish leaves. Dig it up when the leaves have barely begun to appear, prune the straight root short, and plant it in a small container. Plant in soil that is a mixture of red clay with 10 to 20% leaf mold and some river sand.

Growing

When the plant has put out roots, place the container on a shelf and water as with any other plant. Use very weak liquid fertilizer once a week until autumn. Do not apply too much fertilizer. Try not to let the plant to grow too large, but rather encourage a compact shape. In mid-summer, keep it out of the afternoon sun.

Nipping your new Keyaki

The technique of nipping differs in the case of growing trees with straight trunks, depending on whether you want the branches to grow in the form of tiers or in the shape of a broom. In the following paragraphs, the method of growing the branches into a broom-like shape will be explained, as this shape is the best suited for Keyaki.

Let the terminal bud grow into a shoot 15 to 21 cm (6 to 8½ inches) long. By this stage there will be leaves growing along the shoot, and these will get larger as they get nearer the tip. Alongside some of the large leaves will be healthy and vigorous buds. Leave one or two large leaves that are growing near the base (at the point which corresponds to one-third or one-fourth of the desired height), and make a cut at that point. This will encourage the growth of more branches, which should also be trimmed in the same manner after they appear.

If you trim the terminal bud like this, three to four lateral-buds will appear the following spring around the place where the cut was made. From these, select the buds that will become the first, the second, and the third branches; these will eventually form the basis of the tree's shape. Then arrange the branches accordingly. Nev-er allow more than two or three buds, which will eventually become branches, to grow out of one place, since this would make the bonsai look clustered.

Cold-proof shelter

If you leave your Keyaki planted in its small container, outdoors in winter, you run the risk of withering the tips of the buds. To avoid this, put your plant into a shelter early. Take care that it is not humid inside the shelter and ensure that the soil in the container doesn't dry out.

Transplanting

In the following spring, before the buds come out, transplant your bonsai into a larger container. When transplanting, remove approximately half of the old

Aka-Shide (Loose-Flowered Hornbeam)

soil and replace it with new soil that is 7 parts red clay, 2 parts leaf mold, and 1 part coarse sand.

Care after transplanting

Care is basically the same as for the previous year. As for fertilizer, use a very weak liquid solution instead of water two or three times a week. Use a stronger solution once a week, starting in midsummer and continuing until autumn.

Nipping

After the second year, leaves will grow on the branches that have developed from the buds. Leave two or three leaves near the base of the branch and nip the buds of the remaining leaves. This is done to encourage the development of smaller branches and to shape the tips of the branches into a 'broom-like' shape. Repeat this process every time new buds appear. The aim of shaping the bonsai in this manner is to imitate the beautiful flowing lines of a wild Keyaki tree. Bearing this aim in mind, watch the growth of the branches, and try to make sure that all the branches are of the same thickness.

Arranging by wiring

If you don't wire the new twigs that you plan to grow into branches, their tips will begin to droop before the wood part of the twig has hardened, and this will lead to poor growth. To maintain the vitality of the tree, wire the twigs as soon as they start drooping so that they point upwards. Use wire wrapped in paper.

How to develop the roots

The development of the roots is particularly important in growing Keyaki with a single straight trunk. The first step to improving root development is to expose the plant to plenty of sunshine and to apply fertilizer. The second step is to cover and protect the exposed roots with sphagnum moss.

Usually if there is a thick branch on one side of the tree, there will also be a thick root on that same side, which creates a balance between the parts of the tree that are above ground and those which are underground. So, to expand the roots in all directions, arrange the branches so that they spread in all directions too.

Leaf-cutting

Once your tree has grown into its desired shape, you will be cutting the leaves in order to increase the number of branches, and to ensure smaller and denser leaves. Leaf-cutting may be done three times

a year on a very vigorous tree, but usually it is done only twice.

The first cutting should be done when the new twigs have reached a length of 12 to 15 cm (5 to 6 inches). Two weeks before you cut the leaves, nip the tips of the new twigs. This will stop the branches from growing longer, and will broaden the leaves and stimulate the growth of the lateral buds. Cut off all the leaves, leaving only the stems.

The second cutting should be done about 6 weeks later. This time there is no need to nip the new twigs, just cut the leaves. Leaf-cutting is a drastic operation, only to be undertaken if your tree is in perfect health. Take care not to weaken the tree. Other trees that can be treated in the same manner as Keyaki are Aka-Shide (Loose-Flower Hornbeam) Nire-Keyaki (Chinese Elm), and Enoki (Japanese Hackberry).

Kuma-Shide (*Carpinus carpinoides* Makino) Aka-Shide (Loose-Flowered Hornbeam)

Characteristics

Kuma-Shide is related to Aka-Shide or Soro. Their particular feature is their peculiarly shaped catkins. The bracts of flowers on Kuma-Shide are 4–5 cm (1½–2 inches) long and oval-shaped, whereas Aka-Shide bears bracts of flowers that are about 4 cm (1½ inches) long and oblong in shape. The catkins of both Kuma-Shide and Aka-Shide are green, but when exposed to the sun they can become faintly reddened. These catkins fall from the branches in a very elegant way. The plants bear numerous catkins that last a long time. Both trees have large coarse leaves. Those of Kuma-Shide turn crimson in autumn, while the leaves of Aka-Shide are dense and delicate and turn yellow in autumn.

Both are hardy plants, suitable for bonsai. Usually, these trees are grown into straight single trees, but they can also be grown in combination with rocks. Both are easy to grow, long-lived, and beautiful to look at in spring when the buds come out, in autumn when the leaves change color and also in winter when the branches are bare.

Type of tree to use as bonsai

Any variety of Kuma-Shide or Aka-Shide would be suitable for bonsai.

Care

Cut short the straight root, trim the trunk and branches, then plant the tree in a small container in soil that is 80% red clay and 20% coarse sand. The best place for the container and the technique of watering are the same as those described for Keyaki.

About three weeks after transplanting into the container, start giving your plant very weak liquid fertilizer once a week instead of water. Continue this until autumn. Once the leaves have hardened, nip those shoots that have grown too long. In the first year, however, let all the shoots grow long as this will stimulate the development of the roots. In winter, protect from cold.

Transplanting

Transplant every year, in spring before the buds come out. The best soil for transplanting is a mixture of 5 parts black loam, 3 parts red clay and 2 parts coarse sand. Another possible mixture is 7 parts red clay to 2 of leaf mold and 1 of coarse sand. Overgrown branches should be trimmed to maintain a balance within the total appearance of the tree.

Care after transplanting is generally the same as for the year before, except you may use a stronger solution of liquid fertilizer. In addition, solid fertilizer can sometimes be deposited on the soil instead of liquid fertilizer. When the tree has grown into a definite shape, feed it an increased amount of phosphate and potash to stimulate flower-bearing.

Nipping

Nipping should not be done on a weak tree, but on a healthy tree it may be done two to three times in early spring and again in midsummer. Always remember to leave 2 to 3 leaves near the base of the branch and make the cut on the part of the branch right above the highest of the leaves.

Arranging by wiring

Although new twigs and young branches may be scarred by wiring, the scars can be healed by arranging the branches. To avoid permanent damage, use copper or aluminum wire, wrapped in paper.

Leaf-cutting

Leaf-cutting should generally be avoided in Kuma-Shide as it can reduce the number of flowers your plant will bear. In the case of Aka-Shide however — a tree that is grown for the enjoyment of the new buds in spring and for its autumnal tints — it should be encouraged in a tree that is healthy and has not yet bloomed. With such trees, syringe the leaves both after leaf-cutting and during midsummer as a precaution against leaf-burn and to clean the leaves.

Kuma-Shide (*Carpinus carpinoides* Makino)

Trimming the branches

The branches should be trimmed at the same time as transplanting. However, as the flower catkins appear at the tips of the new twigs, leave the branches long until you can tell whether they will bear any flowers. Then cut to a suitable length.

Buna (Japanese Beech)

Characteristics

Although this is a deciduous tree, it does not become completely bare. Brown, withered leaves remain on the tree throughout the winter, only falling when the new, sharply pointed buds appear. This characteristic makes it a favorite with many bonsai-growers. It is hardy, long-lived, and easy to grow.

Varieties

Of the many varieties of Buna, the species best suited for growing as bonsai is Inu-Buna (*Fagus japonica*). Inu-Buna are further divided into two kinds, those with green buds and those with red. The leaves can be variously shaped—round, small, large, spear-shaped and some shaped like those of bamboo. The best type has red buds and small round leaves.

Type of tree to use as bonsai

Both seedlings and trees obtained by layering can be used, although traditionally a young tree or a sapling

Buna (Japanese Beech) showing the fine bark of the trunk.

Buna (Japanese ▶ Beech), Yose-ue (Cluster of trees)

uprooted from the mountains was the common choice. In the case of a young tree, even before you uproot it, cut its trunk off to a height of about 30 cm (12 inches) and trim its branches.

Transplanting

The best soil for transplanting has equal parts of coarse sand and black loam. Choose a deep container, putting coarse soil at the bottom, less coarse soil in the middle, and finer soil at the top, to ensure good drainage. Transplant in spring before the buds emerge.

Care

Place the container on an outdoor shelf in spring and autumn. In midsummer, put it somewhere cool where it will get two or three hours of morning sun, and move it to a shady place for the rest of the day. In winter, put the container in a shelter to protect it against the cold.

Give it plenty of water all the time. The water should be sprinkled on the leaves from the time the leaves harden until the end of summer. Give the tree both liquid and solid fertilizer made from rapeseed cake from the time the buds appear in spring until the middle of autumn. With lack of either fertilizer

or water, the leaves will not last until winter. However, be careful not to apply too much fertilizer as this can cause the plant to wither.

Tree shape

The best shape for this type of tree is straight. By nature, Buna does not develop very strong roots, so you will get a better result if the trees are planted with rocks or in groups.

Planting with rocks

Select a shapely and stable rock—one that has cracks, grooves, and hollows. A medium-sized rock which is easy to handle is preferable. Select a tree that has long fine roots.

Prepare a mixture of clay and sphagnum moss and use it to cover the hollow in the rock where the tree is to be planted. Next, divide the roots into three bunches, place the plant over the hollow, and tie the roots firmly to the rock with twine. Then insert each of the three bunches of roots into the grooves in the rock, starting at the top and working downward. When the roots are inserted in the grooves, cover the rock with the same soil mixture and tie with twine.

After planting the tree on the rock, place it, rock and all, in a flat container in an artistic manner. Put plenty of coarse sand at the very bottom of the container, then cover this with a layer of the clay and sphagnum moss mixture. The lower ends of the longer roots should be buried in the soil. Apply a thick coating of sphagnum moss to those that are too short to reach the soil.

After planting the tree, give plenty of water to the entire plant. Keep the container in semi-shade until the roots are fully developed, and in the meantime syringe the leaves frequently with water.

Nipping

As the new buds of Buna grow vigorously, overgrown buds should be nipped. If the shoots are left unnipped, the internodes will become very long, and warts tend to develop at places where cuts have been made. So make sure to nip the young shoots only once while they are still soft, leaving just one or two leaves. This plant will not produce secondary buds.

Leaf-cutting

It is safer not to cut the leaves during the growing stage of the tree. Even in the case of a tree that has attained its permanent shape, it is dangerous to cut the leaves every year. Cutting the leaves once every other year or so is sufficient.

Arranging the branches by wiring

The bark of this tree is so soft and the branches so quick to grow that you must use wire wrapped in paper when wiring, and be sure to remove all the wire three months after wiring at the latest. As wiring has a negative effect on the tree's ability to absorb water, keep it in the shade, and spray the underside of the leaves with water.

Trimming the branches

A tree that has been transplanted should have its branches trimmed, but trimming too many branches will cause it to wither. It is better to prevent excessive growth and so avoid the need for trimming by nipping the buds while they are still soft.

Transplanting

Transplant every year in the spring. In the case of a tree planted on a rock, however, transplanting is only necessary once every two or three years. Other trees that may be treated in the same manner as Buna are Nara (Small-Leafed Oak), Kunugi (Chestnut-Leafed Oak) and Kashiwa (Daimyo Oak).

Ichō (Maidenhair or Gingko Tree)

Characteristics

Ichō is one of the rare gymnosperms of which there is only one species in one genus in one family. Some specimens are over a thousand years old. It is well known for the fact that there are both male and female plants, and the pollen from the male plant is required to fertilize the female plant. It is extremely difficult to reproduce the aged appearance of this tree in a container in the form of bonsai, but it is possible to encourage it to bear nuts the size of cherries or to develop aerial roots, which will hang like stalactites from the branches just as they do in full-sized trees. The sight of the tree in autumn, when its fan-shaped leaves turn yellow, is indeed beautiful. This is why Ichō is considered one of the most outstanding specimens for bonsai.

Type of tree to use as bonsai

Bonsai can be grown from seedlings, cuttings, grafted trees, and trees obtained by root-grafting. The advantage of using a seedling is that you will be able to enjoy its autumn display from the second year. But if you want your tree to develop aerial roots, it will take at least thirty years of patient and hard labor. However, with the method of root-grafting, it is possible to have stalactitic aerial roots in about four to five years.

If you want your tree to bear nuts, you must obtain a female tree. If you grow your bonsai from a female seedling, you will have to wait about twenty years, but if the method of grafting is used, it could start to fruit after a mere two or three years.

Different Ichō have different leaves, large and small, and some have round nuts and others oblong. Some trees bear nuts in abundance while others do not. Some develop numerous stalactitic aerial roots and others only a few. So when selecting a your tree, be sure to take great care.

Some people have their hearts set on growing an Ichō bonsai that will have beautiful yellow leaves, bear many nuts and have numerous stalactitic aerial roots. Unfortunately, as our technical knowledge currently stands, it is not possible to breed such an ideal bonsai. At present, there are two kinds of bonsai Ichō: one with beautiful yellow leaves and stalactitic aerial roots, and one that bears nuts.

Care

The soil for planting should have equal parts of black loam and red clay. There should be a layer of coarse sand at the bottom, and the soil should become finer toward the surface of the container. This will ensure good drainage. From the time of planting until the roots develop, there is a real threat of root decay. This can be prevented by keeping your plant out of heavy rain and by giving it only a little water.

Where to keep your bonsai and how to water it are basically the same as for any other bonsai. The main exception to these factors is due to the plant's susceptibility to leafburn in midsummer. This jeopardizes the yellowing of the leaves in autumn, but can be prevented by placing the container where it will get a couple of hours of morning sun and shade in the afternoon. Also expose the plant to plenty of dew at night. In places that are subject to dust and fumes from traffic, be sure to syringe the leaves frequently in midsummer to clean the branches, trunk and leaves.

Ichō characteristically has great vitality and responds well to large amounts of fertilizer, provided that the fertilizer is not too strong. Throughout both the growing season and the cold season you should regularly substitute weak liquid fertilizer for water. Somewhat stronger solutions should be given once or twice.

If you want your tree to have a display of yellow leaves in autumn, apply rapeseed cake in liquid form. But if you are aiming for nuts or aerial roots, give your plant fish or bone meal instead.

The shape of the tree and arranging the branches

In nature, Ichō grow into huge trees that reach high up to the sky. So, even in the case of bonsai, it is wiser to develop a tree shape that will resemble its natural form, although this can lead to very tall bonsai of over 60 cm (24 inches). To keep your tree small while still encouraging a natural shape, nip the top annually to stop it from growing too tall, and encourage the branches to become dense in proportion to the height of the tree.

Nipping

Both unwanted new buds and any buds springing from near the roots should be pulled off from the base as soon as they appear. Nip the terminal buds when the leaves have more or less hardened, leaving two or three leaves. When the secondary buds appear, these too should be nipped, leaving two or three leaves out of every four or five. New shoots which you decide to make into branches should be allowed to grow until the leaves have more or less hardened. Then only their tips should be nipped.

All other shoots should be nipped repeatedly, leaving only two leaves out of every three or four. However, after the second nipping, no more nipping should be done after the new twigs have hardened as the cuts will not heal properly, and the branches will wither in winter.

Trimming the branches

Trim branches every spring when you transplant. Making sure you keep the tree looking balanced overall, remove all unnecessary branches and cut the remaining ones to the proper length. When cutting off a branch, be sure to leave a healthy bud under each branch that has been cut.

Ichō (Maidenhair Tree)

Transplanting

Transplant every spring when the new buds appear as dots of green. Sometimes coarse sand can be mixed in the soil, but too much will hamper the growth of the root system and invite sparse branch growth. It is therefore better to use leaf mold instead of sand. The proportion should be 5 parts red clay to 5 of black loam and 2 of leaf mold.

Arranging by wiring and leaf-cutting

Neither of these operations should be done on Ichō.

How to make the yellow leaves in autumn beautiful

Place the plant where there is plenty of fresh air, and let it keep its thick green leaves until as late in autumn as possible.

How to make the plant bear numerous stalactitic aerial roots

Select a tree of the variety that characteristically bears stalactitic aerial roots. Everything else depends on the patient care bestowed on the plant.

How to make the plant bear nuts

Select a tree that belongs to the strain that bears many nuts. Give it plenty of fertilizer that is rich in phosphate and potash. The most important and difficult thing is to leave the tree in the neighborhood of a male tree. However, as the pollen of Ichō is very minute, it scatters like mist over a distance of more than 30 km. Accordingly, if there are any male trees within this radius, you should not need to search for one closer to hand.

Karin (Chinese Quince)

Characteristics

Of all deciduous trees that are grown as bonsai, there is perhaps none so hardy and long-lived as Karin. It has a hard trunk and smooth bark. As a young tree it is not particularly imposing, but its grandeur increases with age. The bark alone is a feature to enjoy, as it becomes attractively mottled with age. The branches too are a genuine feature. Its leaves are rather large, and although the tree does not bear many flowers, the large elliptical yellow fruits that ripen on the branches after the leaves have fallen are truly a sight to be seen. When these fruits are ripe they emit a sweet fragrance. This species suits many styles of bonsai, and can be grown with equal success as a bonsai with a single straight trunk, with a slant-

ing trunk, or in the semi-cascade style. It is not particularly difficult to grow. Some claim that the tree does not bear many fruits, but, given appropriate fertilizer and trimmed correctly it will certainly contradict such a claim.

Type of tree to use as bonsai

Karin develop roots easily, so it is easy to obtain a tree by layering. The best time for layering is when the new buds begin to grow. Peel the bark around the place where you wish to cut off the branch, wrap the area with water-soaked sphagnum moss, and keep watering the moss so that it is always moise. After about three weeks, roots will develope. In two months, the branch will be ready to separate from the parent tree. If the tree obtained by layering has a trunk or a branch with a diameter of 3 to 5 cm (1½ to 2 inches), it can be cut off after half a year and then grown as bonsai.

Care

If you choose a Karin for your bonsai, your aim will be to enjoy the beauty of the tree when it bears its golden fruit. To ensure this, you must take pains to grow a good healthy tree with a properly arranged shape. Plant it in soil that is 4 parts black loam, 3 red clay, 2 Kanuma soil, and 1 coarse sand.

The soil should both hold and drain water well. Trim all unnecessary branches, and then plant firmly so that it will not move. Place the container where it will get plenty of sunshine and fresh air.

As the plant has large leaves it will need plenty of water. Never allow your plant to suffer from a lack of

Karin (Chinese Quince) of fruit being cultivated on a roof.

water. While the tree is young, fertilize with rapeseed cake both as a weak liquid and deposited on the soil in a solid form, as the tree needs it.

Nipping

Nip all unnecessary buds as soon as they appear. Allow the new buds that you want to develop into branches to grow until their leaves have more or less hardened. Then nip just their tips. Other shoots that you want to grow into small branches should be stopped from growing once they are between 4 and 6 cm (1½ and 2½ inches) long. To do this, delay nipping until their leaves have begun to harden, then leave just one or two leaves. This will cause the secondary buds to come out. These should again be nipped like the primary buds. Tertiary buds should also be nipped.

If you repeat nipping this way, your Karin, which is a very vigorous tree, will only develop a few main branches, will have many smaller branches, and won't grow too tall. To arrange the branches properly, also thin out young shoots that have grown too densely.

Arranging the branches by wiring

Use wire wrapped with paper when arranging the new twigs. Wiring should be done at the same time as nipping. When wiring, take care not to snap the new twigs, as they will be soft and easily broken at this time.

The best time to arrange the one, two and three-year old branches by wiring is early in the spring, just before the buds come out. Here again it is best to use wire wrapped in paper. It is better not to wire the old branches or the trunk. The wires should be removed in the autumn of the same year so that they don't cut into the bark.

Cold-proof measures

Karin resists the cold well, but because it requires repeated nipping there is a danger that the tips of its branches will wither in the winter. To prevent this, put your plant in a frost-proof shelter.

Trimming the branches

Trim withered and overgrown branches early in the spring before the buds come out, but be sure to maintain the harmony and balance of the tree. If you wish to remove any thicker branches, do not remove them all at once. Such branches should be cut off over a period of two or three years, cutting them a little shorter every year.

Transplanting

Transplant every spring before the buds come out. The buds of Karin appear earlier in the spring than with other deciduous trees, so be careful to transplant at the right time. The tree grows so vigorously that its roots will fill the container in one year. Therefore, when transplanting, prune the roots closely.

Fertilizing to stimulate fruit-bearing

Once the tree has assumed a more or less definite shape, rapeseed cake alone will not provide sufficient nutrition. So you should also give your plant a weak liquid fertilizer, made from bone meal or fish bones, or a small amount of superphosphate, and from time to time it is a good idea to deposit solid fertilizer on the soil. As Karin is susceptible to a potash deficiency during the growing season, give your tree a solution of wood ash now and then.

But do not give it any fertilizer during the flowering season or after the fruit has appeared. Watering alone is sufficient during this period.

Relationship between nipping and the bearing of fruits

In the case of Karin, it is necessary to nip the buds repeatedly. For other deciduous trees, repeated nipping generally jeopardizes the development of branches with the consequence that no flower-buds form. And if the blossoms are poor, it follows that the fruit will be inferior. However, Karin is an exception, in that, if sufficient fertilizer is given, nipping can be repeated several times without any ill effects.

Picking the fruits and cautions to be observed in summer

Karin bear large fruit. If a tree is allowed to bear too many fruit at one time, it will become exhausted and will not bear any fruit the next year. So when a good number of fruit has appeared on the tree and they are about the size of nuts, thin them out, leaving only a few that are well-developed and in good positions.

If you allow the fruit that are left to be exposed to the strong afternoon sun in midsummer, you risk turning the fruit black from sunburn. They may even drop off before they are fully developed. So take care to protect your tree from the afternoon sun in midsummer. Lastly, if ripe fruit is left on the tree until it drops, the tree will lose its vitality. It is therefore best to pick the fruit at a suitable time.

VI

BRIEF DESCTIPTION OF THE GROWING TECHNIQUES FOR BONSAI

Needle-Leafed Evergreens

AKA-MATSU (Japanese Red Pine)
When to transplant: In spring after the appearance of the buds.
How often to transplant: Once every three to four years.
Soil: 70% red clay, 30% coarse sand.
Watering: Do not overwater. Syringe the leaves in mid-summer.
Fertilizer: Deposit rapeseed-cake fertilizer about three times during the growing season.
Nipping: As for Kuro-Matsu (Japanese Black Pine).
Arranging by wiring: As for Kuro-Matsu (Japanese Black Pine).
Other points to bear in mind: Remove old leaves by hand after midsummer. Trim all unnecessary branches at the time of transplanting.

Aka-Matsu (Japanese Red Pine) Seedling tree.

Kara-Matsu (Japanese Larch)

KARA-MATSU (Japanese Larch)

When to transplant: In spring before the buds sprout.

How often to transplant: Once every three to four years.

Soil: 50% red clay, 50% coarse sand.

Watering: Take care to apply the right amount of water. Give plenty of water straight after transplanting, during the spring budding season and in midsummer.

Fertilizer: Avoid excessive fertilizing. Deposit rapeseed-cake twice when the new twigs are growing.

Nipping: Wait until side-buds appear next to the new twigs, then nip the twigs if they have grown too long, leaving one or two side-buds near the base.

Arranging by wiring: Avoid wiring the trunk or thick branches, as the bark is soft and may be damaged by wire. Wire new twigs with wire wrapped in paper.

Other points to bear in mind: Protect against cold in winter. Prune all unnecessary branches at the time of transplanting. Do not let the roots become moldy.

KOME-TSUGA (Japanese Northern Hemlock)

When to transplant: During spring budding time.

How often to transplant: Once every three to four years.

Soil: 40–50% red clay, 50–60% coarse sand.

Watering: Not much is needed, but the leaves should be syringed thoroughly at budding time and in summer.

Fertilizer: Apply very weak liquid fertilizer two or three times in spring at budding time. After that, deposit rapeseed cake once or twice during the growing season.

Nipping: Nip the buds once after the leaves have more or less hardened.

Arraanging by wiring: Bare wire may be applied in spring, but avoid tight wiring.

Other points to bear in mind: Unnecessary branches should be trimmed when wiring the tree.

ONKŌ (Japanese Yew) and KAYA (*Torrela nucifera*)

These may both be treated as for Kome-Tsuga (Japanese Northern Hemlock). However, strong sunshine is bad for Onkō, so keep it out of direct summer sun.

HINOKI (Hinoki Cypress) and TSUKUMO-HIBA (Dwarf Form of Sawara Cypress)

When to transplant: Early spring.

How often to transplant: Every other year.

Soil: 50% black loam, 20% leaf mold, 30% coarse sand.

Watering: Give plenty of water. Leaves need practically no watering.

Fertilizer: As for Shimpaku (Chinese Juniper).

Nipping: Nip the buds with the fingers in spring and autumn when the new buds come out. Twice in spring and once in autumn should be enough.

Arranging by wiring: Wiring should be done in early spring.

Other points to bear in mind: In warm climates, prune unwanted branches in autumn. In other climates, prune at the same time as wiring.

SAWARA (Sawara Cypress)

Treat as for Hinoki (Hinoki Cypress), but use liquid fertilizer and, in summer, syringe the leaves.

KONOTE-KASHIWA (Chinese Arborvitae)

When to transplant: Early spring.

How often to transplant: Once every two to three years.

Soil: 50% red clay, 20% black loam, 30% coarse sand.

Watering: Avoid overwatering. In summer, expose the plant to dew at night.

Fertilizer: Deposit rapeseed-cake fertilizer three to four times during the growing season.

Nipping: Nip three times a year, as with Hinoki (Hinoki Cypress).

Arranging by wiring: Wire, using bare wire, early in spring before budding time. As the branches and leaves of Konote-Kashiwa tend to grow rather large for bonsai, wiring is necessary to shape the tree by changing the distribution of the branches and leaves. Wiring should be done before the leaves grow too large.

Other points to bear in mind: This is a very hardy tree which can withstand extremes of heat, cold and dryness. It is, however, susceptible to damp.

Flowering Deciduous Trees

RŌBAI (Beeswax Flower)

When to transplant: After the flowering season.

How often to transplant: Every one to two years.

Soil: 60% black loam, 30% Kanuma soil, 10% coarse sand.

Watering: Water as for Ume (Flowering Japanese Apricot) .

Fertilizer: As for Ume (Flowering Japanese Apricot), use a weak liquid fertilizer with organic fertilizer.

Nipping: Nip off all unwanted new buds as they appear. New shoots should be trimmed in midsummer as seems necessary.

Arranging by wiring: Wiring old branches is a difficult task, so wait until the bark has become soft first and use wire wrapped in paper to prevent hurting the branches. Use wire wrapped in paper for new twigs.

Other points to bear in mind: As Robai is susceptible to cold, take it indoors early in winter. Prune the branches to an appropriate length, carefully observing the condition of the flower buds in late autumn or early spring in order to prevent them from overgrowing and thereby making the tree look unkempt. When transplanting, take care not to prune the roots too closely. In summer, do not expose the plant to the strong afternoon sun.

ŌBAI (Winter Jasmine)

When to transplant: Either in autumn after the leaves have fallen, or in spring before the flowers bloom.
How often to transplant: Once a year.
Soil: As for Rōbai (Beeswax flower).
Watering: Expose to plenty of sunshine all year round and water the roots whenever the soil dries out.
Fertilizer: Use liquid fertilizer from the end of the flowering season until autumn. The best fertilizer is rapeseed cake mixed either with bone meal or with a small amount of superphosphate.
Nipping: Nip off all unnecessary new shoots before they grow too large. Allow the remaining new shoots to grow long, cutting them to a suitable length when the lower portions of the new twigs begin to harden.
Arranging by wiring: Use wire wrapped in paper after nipping.
Other points to bear in mind: As Ōbai has a tendency to root from its nodes, be sure to cut off any roots springing from the branches. These roots tend to develop during the tree's growing season and also during the Japanese rainy season (in late spring). Therefore, it is advisable to keep your bonsai out of the rain during the rainy season. Cut any overgrown branches to a suitable length before the flowering season and according to the condition of the flower buds, which should be observed in order to prevent them from overgrowing.

SANZASHI (Chinese Hawthorn)

When to transplant: In spring before the buds sprout.
How often to transplant: Once.
Soil: 60% black loam, 20% red clay, 20% coarse sand.
Watering: Give plenty of water.
Fertilizer: During the growing season, apply weak liquid fertilizer twice a month. For trees that bear berries, however, apply instead a rather strong liquid fertilizer containing phosphate and potash in the second half of the same period.
Nipping: Nip off the tips of the shoots when the leaves of the new buds have begun to harden.
Arranging by wiring: Use wire wrapped in paper when the new shoots have begun to harden. Remove the wire in autumn.
Other points to bear in mind: Prune the branches either after the tree has flowered or after the berries appear. If there are too many berries, they should be thinned out before falling naturally, otherwise the tree will become weak.

KAIDŌ (Showy Crab Apple)

When to transplant: In spring before the buds sprout.
How often to transplant: Once.
Soil: 70% black loam, 10% Kanuma soil, 20% coarse sand.
Watering: Give plenty of water.
Fertilizer: As with Sanzashi (Chinese Hawthorn), there are two kinds of Kaidō. One is grown for its flowers, and the other for its fruit. The method of fertilizer application is the same as for Sanzashi (Chinese Hawthorn).
Nipping: Allow the new buds to grow for a little, then nip the tips.
Arranging by wiring: Use wire wrapped in paper when the new shoots begin to harden.
Other points to bear in mind: If there is a lot of fruit, you must pick it before it drops naturally or the tree will become weak. Large scars on the branches or trunk should be carved in winter. Tie sphagnum moss to the carved area to hasten the healing process.

SAKURA (Flowering Cherry)

When to transplant: In spring before the buds sprout.
How often to transplant: Every year.
Soil: Equal parts of black loam, red clay, and coarse sand.
Watering: Water sparingly except in the case of the alpine Fuji-Zakura (*Prunus incisa*), which requires occasional syringing of the leaves.
Fertilizer: This tree is sensitive to fertilizer, so avoid using an organic fertilizer. Apply very weak liquid fertilizer made from rapeseed cake several times during the growing season.
Nipping: Trim the branches after flowering, leaving two or three nodes. Nip the tips of the new buds when the leaves have begun to harden.
Arranging by wiring: Use wire wrapped in paper at about the same time as you nip the buds. Remove the wires in autumn.
Other points to bear in mind: Trim all unnecessary branches when you transplant. But do not tamper too much with the branches. Eradicate insects upon discovery.

MOKUREN (Lily Magnolia) and KOBUSHI (Kobushi Magnolia, yulan)

When to transplant: Immediately after the flowering season.
How often to transplant: Every year.
Soil: 60% black loam, 20–30% red clay, and 10–20% coarse sand.
Watering: Give plenty of water. In summer, place the container in a cool, shady place where it will get only two to three hours of morning sun.
Fertilizer: Application of fertilizer should be concentrated in the first half of the growing season (April and

May). Liquid fertilizer should be applied two or three times a month in July, September and October, or during the peak of summer and autumn.

Nipping: As this tree will not grow a profusion of branches, only remove those new buds which are unwanted. When the leaves have hardened, nip the remaining buds to a suitable length.

Arranging by wiring: Use wire wrapped in paper at the same time as nipping. Remove the wires in autumn.

Other points to bear in mind: As the flowers tend to bloom with their backs to the sun, move the container now and then.

Sakura (Flowering Cherry)

ZAIFURI-BOKU (Japanese Juneberry)
When to transplant: In spring before the buds sprout.
How often to transplant: Annually.
Soil: 50% black loam, 30% red clay, 10% leaf mold and 10% coarse sand.
Watering: Water the leaves in spring when the buds sprout. Afterwards, give plenty of water during the growing season.
Fertilizer: Apply liquid fertilizer twice a month during the growing season. Start with very weak fertilizer during the first half of the season, gradually making it stronger through the second half. During the second half of the growing season, however, fertilize less frequently.
Nipping: Trim the branches after the flowering season. Let the new buds grow until the leaves have begun to harden, then nip their tips.
Other points to bear in mind: As the branches of this tree do not ramify greatly, do not prune them too closely.

ZAKURO (Pomegranate)
When to transplant: About the time the new buds begin to open their leaves in spring.
How often to transplant: Either once a year, or once every two years.
Soil: 50% black loam, 10% leaf mold, 20% Kanuma soil, and 20% coarse sand.
Watering: This tree must have a container with good drainage. Make sure it gets plenty of sunshine and water. Leave outdoors, even in summer. Expose to the dew at night.
Fertilizer: Use decomposed liquid fertilizer made from rapeseed cake mixed with bone meal or fish-bones. Apply weak fertilizer three to four times a month during the first half of the growing season. During the second half, apply gradually stronger fertilizer twice a month.
Nipping: Nip the new shoots when they reach a height of 9 to 12cm (3½ to 5 inches), leaving 1 to 2 nodes. Nip the secondary buds when they reach a height of 7 to 8 cm (3 to 3½ inches), leaving one node.
Arranging by wiring: Wire every second year, using wire wrapped in paper, at the same time as nipping.
Other points to bear in mind: If there are too many flower buds at the tips of the new twigs, thin them out. Pick the new fruit before it falls off the tree to prevent the tree from becoming weak.

SARUSUBERI or HYAKUJIKKO (Crape Myrtle)
When to transplant: In spring around budding time.
How often to transplant: Every year.
Soil: 80% black loam, 20% coarse sand.
Watering: Water the roots as for any other plant. Water the leaves during budding time.
Fertilizer: As the plant is slow to sprout buds and quick to lose leaves, be sure to give sufficient liquid fertilizer and organic manure from the time the roots develop

until midsummer.

Nipping: Prune the branches closely before the buds sprout. Nip the new buds both when the flower buds begin to sprout and once flowering is over.

Arranging by wiring: Do this at midsummer, using wire wrapped in paper.

Other points to bear in mind: The tree will not bear many flowers if nipped too early and too often. Protect from cold in winter.

NEMU-NO-KI (Silk Tree)

When to transplant:
In spring before the buds sprout.

How often to transplant: Every two years.

Soil: 50% black loam, 20% red clay, 10% leaf mold, and 20% coarse sand.

Watering: Give plenty of water. In summer, place where it will get two to three hours of morning sun and shade for the rest of the day. Expose to the dew at night.

Fertilizer: During the growing season, apply liquid fertilizer once every ten days or so. Occasionally add some wood ash solution to the liquid fertilizer.

Nipping: Do not nip the new twigs too close to the base. Nip after transplanting has been completed and the flowering season is over. Only nip the tips of the buds that must be removed to
retain the shape of the tree.

Arranging by wiring: As for Sarusuberi (Crape Myrtle).

Other points to bear in mind: Trim the branches at the same time as transplanting and after the flowering season. In winter protect from the cold.

Flowering Evergreens

TSUBAKI (Camellias)

When to transplant: The best time is after the flowering season, whether it is a variety that blooms in winter or in spring. Do not transplant during the cold weather in winter.

How often to transplant: For young trees, transplant every two years; for a mature tree with a finished shape, transplant every three years.

Soil: 70% to black loam, 30% red clay, and 20% coarse sand.

Watering: As for any other plant. Avoid exposure to strong afternoon sunlight from the time the leaves start to harden until summer. Water the leaves frequently.

Fertilizer: Apply liquid fertilizer twice a month during the growing season. During the second half of this season, also give a generous amount of phosphate and potash. Young trees in particular require sufficient fertilizer.

Nipping: Nip the tips of the shoots when the leaves begin to harden. Trim the tips of the branches after the

flower buds have formed.

Arranging by wiring: Using wire wrapped in paper, arrange the branches at the time of nipping.

Other points to bear in mind: Thin out the flower buds if there seem to be too many. Prune the branches when you transplant. In winter, keep your plant indoors where there is plenty if light.

SATSUKI (Satsuki Azalea)

When to transplant: After the flowering season.

How often to transplant: Transplant young trees every year, and older trees every two years.

Soil: 60–70% Kanuma soil, and 40–30% finely shredded sphagnum moss.

Watering: Expose to plenty of sunshine, and water the roots well. Syringe the leaves after transplanting until the roots develop, and every morning and evening throughout summer. In summer, put the container in a cool shady spot out of direct sunlight.

Fertilizer: Use weak liquid fertilizer two or three times a month during the growing season. Do not fertilize during the flowering season.

Nipping: Nip all unnecessary buds as soon as they sprout. Nip overgrown new shoots while they are still soft, leaving two or three leaves near the base.

Arranging by wiring: Wiring should be carried out during the growing season. First wrap raffia around the trunk and thick branches, then use wire wrapped in paper.

Other points to bear in mind: When you transplant, also trim off any withered branches and those that have grown too dense. Do this again when you wire the branches. If there are too many flower buds they should be thinned out. After the flowering season, cut off all the withered flowers to prevent them from bearing seeds.

KUCHINASHI (Cape Gardenia)

When to transplant: In spring before the buds appear.

How often to transplant: Once a year.

Soil: 50% to black loam, 30% red clay, and 20% coarse sand.

Watering: Expose to sufficient sunlight. Water sparingly.

Fertilizer: During the growing season, apply weak liquid fertilizer consisting of rapeseed cake and organic fertilizer twice a month.

Nipping: Nip the tips of shoots when the leaves on the new twigs have hardened. Overgrown and withered branches should be pruned when you transplant.

Arranging by wiring: Using wire wrapped in paper, arrange the branches at the same time as nipping.

Other points to bear in mind: Place the container in semi-shade during summer and protect from cold in winter. Remove the fruit before it dries and withers.

HAZE (Japanese Wax Tree)

When to transplant: In spring just before the buds sprout.

How often to transplant: Every year.

Soil: 50% black loam soil, 20% red clay, 20% leaf mold, and 10% coarse sand.

Watering: As for any other tree, but do not overwater. Syringe the leaves in midsummer.

Fertilizer: Apply fertilizer twice a month in April and May. Apply only once a month in September and October. Use liquid fertilizer about twice a month.

Nipping: Nip the new shoots when they are fully grown, leaving two or three leaves near the base.

Arranging by wiring: Wire new twigs in summer using wire wrapped in paper. Wire older branches in spring before the buds come out.

Other points to bear in mind: In summer, do not expose the plant to the afternoon sun; protect from cold in winter.

NISHIKI-GI (Winged Spindle Tree) and Mayumi (Japanese Strawberry Bush)

When to transplant: In spring about the time the buds sprout.

How often to transplant: Every year.

Soil: As for Haze (Japanese Wax Tree).

Watering: As for any other plant. In summer, place in semi-shade and water the leaves frequently.

Fertilizer: Since the plant is grown for its autumn colours and berries, use liquid fertilizer made from rapeseed cake mixed with bone meal or a small amount of superphosphate. In the first half of the growing season, apply a weak solution of this fertilizer three times a month. During the second half, apply a slightly stronger solution roughly twice a month.

Nipping: Nip the new shoots, leaving about two buds. Trim overgrown and unwanted branches when transplanting.

Arranging by wiring: Use wire wrapped in paper at the time of nipping.

Other points to bear in mind: Cut off large or soiled leaves just before midsummer.

MEGI (Japanese Barberry)

When to transplant: In spring when the buds appear.

How often to transplant: Every year.

Soil:: 50% black loam, 30% red clay, and 20% coarse sand.

Watering: Give plenty of water. In summer, place in semi-shade and syringe the leaves frequently.

Fertilizer: As for Nishiki-gi (Winged Spindle Tree).

Nipping: Nip two or three times. As flowers will appear beside the leaves on new twigs, let the new shoots grow fairly long before trimming them.

Arranging by wiring: Arrange at the same time as transplanting. Cut off all unwanted branches and use wire wrapped in paper.

Other points to bear in mind: When handling, look out for the sharp thorns.

TSUTA (Japanese Ivy)

When to transplant: In spring before the buds sprout.

How often to transplant: Every year.

Soil: 70% red clay, 20% Kanuma soil, and 10% coarse sand.

Watering: Give plenty of water. Syringe the leaves frequently in summer.

Fertilizer: Use weak liquid fertilizer three times a month during the first half of the growing season.

Nipping: As Tsuta is a climbing plant, to prevent it from becoming overgrown, cut the vines, leaving each of two leaves at the base of each branch, whenever they reach a height of 6 to 9 cm (5½ to 3½ inches). During the rainy season in Japan (in late spring), cut off all leaves from the base, as this will encourage the appearance of fresh new leaves.

Arranging by wiring: Use wire wrapped in paper at the same time as transplanting. Old branches cannot be bent sharply as they are brittle and tend to snap easily.

Other points to bear in mind: Remove any small vines that are growing too densely. Prune all unnecessary or withered branches when you transplant.

SHIRAKABA (Japanese White Birch)

When to transplant: In spring before the buds sprout.

How often to transplant: Every year.

Soil: 60% black loam, 20% red clay, and 20% coarse sand.

Watering: Plant in a container with good drainage, and water generously. In summer, place in semi shade. Give the leaves plenty of water.

Fertilizer: Application of fertilizer should be concentrated in the first half of the growing season. Use very weak decayed liquid fertilizer, consisting of rapeseed cake mixed with bone meal, two or three times a month.

Nipping: As soon as the new shoots have grown, nip their buds once or twice leaving two or three leaves.

Arranging by wiring: Use wire wrapped in paper. Wire when the leaves on the new twigs have begun to harden. Remove the wire in autumn.

Other points to bear in mind: Remove the soiled surface of the old bark every two years. Do not use fertilizer with a high nitrogen content.

YANAGI (Weeping Willow)

When to transplant: In early summer and in midsummer.

How often to transplant: Twice a year.

Soil: 50% black loam, 30% Kanuma soil, and 20% coarse sand.

Watering: Yanagi need a lot of water. In summer, place

in a cool, semi-shaded spot. Keep out of strong sunlight, especially afternoon sun. Syringe the leaves frequently.

Fertilizer: During the growing season, apply very weak liquid fertilizer three times a month.

Trimming the new shoots: Prune the new shoots, leaving two or three nodes, at the time of transplanting. Any new buds appearing after this should be alllowed to grow without nipping.

Arranging by wiring: Yanagi will start to sprout new buds vigorously after the new shoots that were allowed to grow long have been pruned short again. Accordingly, only wire the thick branches in early spring before the buds come out. Use wire wrapped in paper.

Other points to bear in mind: Do not delay the second transplanting. As the roots of this plant develop quickly, it consumes a great deal of water. You may put the container under water for short periods of time from May to August. Do not leave submerged for too long or you may cause an oxygen shortage and root suffocation.

GYORYU (Tamarisk)

When to transplant: In spring about the time the buds sprout.

How often to transplant: Each year.

Soil: As for Yanagi (Weeping Willow).

Watering: and fertilizer: As for Yanagi (Weeping Willow).

Trimming the branches: Trim all branches close at the time of transplanting, making sure the shape of the tree is well balanced. Dense young shoots should be thinned out.

Arranging by wiring: Use paper-wrapped wires for thick branches. Suspending the branches can be used instead of wiring.

Other points to bear in mind: The important thing here is to distribute the young shoots properly. Wiring is one way to ensure good shoot distribution, so that the tree will not look uneven. In order to increase the number of buds, cut off any withered buds as soon as they start opening in mid-April and place the plant in a container filled with water.

Fruiting Deciduous Trees

YUSURA-UME (*Prunus tomentosa*)

When to transplant: In spring before the buds sprout.

How often to transplant: Every year.

Soil: As for Sanzashi (Japanese Hawthorn).

Watering: Expose to plenty of sunshine. Give plenty of water.

Fertilizer: As this tree is grown for its display of flowers and fruit, use a weak liquid fertilizer consisting of

rapeseed cake and bone meal. Apply two or three times a month during the growing season.

Nipping: Nip the tops of the buds of new overgrown shoots. In spring, when you transplant, prune the twigs to a suitable length, as is appropriate in relation to the condition of the buds. As this plant tends to grow buds easily near the roots and the base of the branches, cut them off as soon as they appear.

Arranging by wiring: When wiring young branches, use wire wrapped in paper. Wire them before the buds appear.

Other points to bear in mind: One way to develop a young tree is to thin out the fruits by picking them. As this plant has a very low resistance to chemical preparations, take care when applying insecticide. Protect from the cold in winter.

KAKI (Japanese Persimmon)

When to transplant: In the spring before the buds appear.

How often to transplant: Every year.

Soil: 40% black loam, 30% red clay, 20% leaf mold, and 10% coarse sand.

Watering: Expose to sufficient sunlight, and give plenty of water.

Fertilizer: Use both liquid and organic fertilizer during the growing season. During the second half of the season, use fertilizer that is rich in phosphate and potash.

Nipping: Nip all unnecessary young shoots as soon as possible. Trim the flower buds to a suitable length after they appear on the new twigs. The twigs you have chosen to grow into branches should be allowed to grow until they stop growing in late July. Then cut the ends off and allow their secondary leaves to grow. Nipping should be done when the bonsai is transplanted.

Arranging by wiring: Use wire wrapped in paper. Wire when the leaves have begun to harden. Remove the wires in autumn.

Other points to bear in mind: Protect against the cold in winter. Give the tree a rest once every three years by not allowing the same branches to produce fruit every year. Only 6 to 7 fruits should be left on the tree every time and all the rest should be pruned. The same branches may bear fruit two consecutive years but should be allowed to rest the third year by nipping the buds as soon as they appear. Prune the branches when you transplant.

KURI (Japanese Chestnut)

When to transplant: In spring before the buds sprout.

How often to transplant: Every year.

Soil: 60% black loam, 20% Kanuma soil, and 20% coarse sand.

Watering:: Give plenty of water.

Fertilizer: During the growing season, apply a weak liquid fertilizer made from a mixture of rapeseed cake and bone meal two or three times a month.

Nipping: Nip the tips of young shoots that have grown too long. Nip the tips of the young twigs after the fruit has formed.

Arranging by wiring: Use wire wrapped in paper for young shoots that are still tender.

Other points to bear in mind: In winter, protect against the cold to prevent the branches from withering.

HIME-RINGO (Nagasaki Crab Apple)

When to transplant: In spring around budding time.

How often to transplant: Every year.

Soil: 40% black loam, 20% red clay, 30% Kanuma soil, and 10% coarse sand.

Giving water: As for any other plant.

Fertilizer: During the first half of the growing season apply weak liquid fertilizer made from rapeseed cake and bone meal or fish manure. During the second half, after the fruits have begun to swell, use stronger liquid fertilizer and decrease the number of applications.

Nipping: Nip the tips of the shoots after allowing them to grow a little. Trim the branches at the same time as transplanting.

Arranging by wiring: Using wire wrapped in paper, arrange the branches at the same time as nipping.

Other points to bear in mind: This tree bears numerous fruit, so after enjoying the display for some time, pick them to prevent the tree from becoming weak.

AKEBI (Five-Leaf Akebia)

When to transplant: In spring when the buds appear.

How often to transplant: Every one to two years.

Soil: 40% black loam, 30% red clay, 10% leaf mold, and 20% coarse sand.

Watering: Give plenty of water. Do not expose to direct sunlight in summer. Syringe the leaves occasionally.

Fertilizer: Use liquid fertilizer mixed with organic manure. Use a stronger fertilizer after the fruits have attained their full size.

Nipping: Nip all unwanted new shoots as they appear. Check the growth of overgrown shoots by pulling them downwards.

Arranging by wiring: There is no need for this treatment.

Other points to bear in mind: To make the plant bear plenty of fruit, pollinate artificially. In the time between the opening of the flowers and the formation of the fruit, make sure the tree is out of the wind.

Hime-Ringo (Nagasaki Crab Apple)

Fruiting Evergreens

BUSSHU-KAN (Buddha's hand citron)

When to transplant: In spring around budding time.

How often to transplant: Every one to two years.

Soil: 50% red clay, 30% black loam, and 20% coarse sand.

Watering: Expose to sufficient sunlight, and always give plenty of water.

Fertilizer: Instead of watering, apply plenty of very weak liquid fertilizer, consisting of fish manure or fish manure mixed with bone meal during the growing season (April to October) until the flowers open. Do not fertilize during the rainy season. From the time the fruit begins to swell until it starts to change colour, give a somewhat stronger fertilizer twice a month.

Nipping: Trim the young shoots which have not developed any buds. Keep the ones that have developed buds. In autumn, nip the tips of the secondary shoots.

Arranging by wiring: Arrange the branches by wiring whenever you nip the buds. When doing so, wrap raffia around the old branches.

Other points to bear in mind: In winter, take the plant indoors to protect it from the cold. To make the branches thicken, pick the fruit early and apply pllenty of fretilizer.

Bonsai Species

(Japanese)	(Latin)	(English)
Aka-Ezo-Matsu	*Picea glehni* Mast.	Saghalien Spruce
Aka-Matsu	*Pinus densiflora* Sieb. et Zucc.	Japanese Red Pine
Aka-Shide	*Carpinus laxiflora* Blume	Loose-Flowered Hornbeam
Akebi	*Akebia Quinata* Decne.	Five-Leafed Akebia
Beni-Shitan	*Cotoneaster horizontalis* Dec.	Rock Cotoneaster
Boke	*Chaenomeles* L.	Japanese Flowering Ouince
Kan-Boke	*Chaenomeles speciosa* Nakai	Japanese Flowering Quince
Kusa-Boke	*Chaenomeles japonica* (Thunb.) Lindl.	Lesser Flowering Quince
Yod-Boke 'Toyonishiki'	*Chaenomeles speciosa* Nakai cv. Tōyōnishiki	Japanese Flowering Quince 'Tōyōnishiki'
'Choju-bai'	*Chaenomeles speciosa* Nakai cv. Chojubai	Japanese Flowering Quince 'Choju-bai'
Buna	*Fagus crenata* Blume	Japanese Beech (white)
Inu-Buna, Kuro-Buna	*Fagus japonica* Maxim	Japanese Beech (black)
Bussu-Kan	*Citrus medica* var. *sarcodactylis* Swingle	Buddha's Hand Citron
Cha	*Thea sinensis* L.	Tea-Plant
Enoki	*Celtis sinensis japonica* Pers. var. *japonica* Nakai	Japanese Hackberry
Ezo-Matsu	*Picea jezoensis* Carr.	Ezo Spruce
Kuro-Ezo-Matsu		Yesso Spruce
Fuji	*Wistaria floribunda* (Willd.) DC.	Wisteria
Noda-Fuji	*Wistaria floribunda* (Willd.) DC.	Wisteria
Yama-Fuji	*Wistaria brachybotrys* Sieb. et Zucc.	Wild Wisteria
Goyō-Matsu	*Pinus pentaphylla* Mayr var. *himekomatsu* Makino	Five-Needled Pine
Hai-Matsu	"	Five-Needled Pine 'Hai-Matsu'
Yatsubusa-Goyō	"	Five-Needled Pine with Eight Clusters
Gumi	*Elaeagnus multiflora* Thunb.	Gumi, Goumi
Gyōryu	*Tamarix chinensis* Lour.	Chinese Tamarisk
Hai-byakushin (Sonare)	*Juniperus procunbens* Sieb. et Zucc.	Creeping Japanese Juniper
Hai-Matsu	*Pinus pumila* Regel	Dwarf Stone Pine
Haze	*Rhus succedanea* L.	Japanese Wax Tree
Hime-Ringo	*Malus baccata* Borkh. var. *mandshuria* Schneid.	Nagasaki Crab Apple
Hinoki	*Chamaecyparis obtusa* Sieb. et Zucc.	Hinoki Cypress, Japanese Cypress
Chabo-Hiba	*Chamaaecyparis obtusa* Endl. var. *brevirarmea* Mast.	Dwarf form of Sawara Cypress
Tsukumo-Hiba		
Hyotan-boku	*Lonicera morrowii* A Gray	Morrow Honeysuckle
Ibuki (Byakushin)	*Juniperus chinensis* L. var. *aureo-globosa* Rehd.	Chinese Juniper
Ōgon-Ibuki	*Juniperus chinensis* L. var. *aureo-globosa*	Ōgon Juniper
Tama-Ibuki	*Juniperus chinensis* L. var. *globosa* Hornibr.	Tama Juniper
Kaizuka-Ibuki	*Juniperus chinensis* L. var. Kaizuka hort.	Kaizuka Juniper
Ichō	*Ginkgo biloba* L.	Maidenhair Tree, Gingko Tree
Kaede	*Acer* L.	Japanese Maple
Kaidō	*Malus micromalus* Makino	Kaido Crab Apple
Suishi-Kaidō	*Malus halliana* koehne	Showy Hall's Crab
Kaki	*Diospyros kaki* Thunb.	Japanese Persimmon
Hime-Gaki 'Roa'	*Diospyros rhombifolia* Hemsl.	'Roa' Chinese Persimmon
Yama-Gaki	*Diospyros kaki* Thunb. var. *silvestris* Makino	Wild Persimmon
Kara-Matsu	*Larix leptolepis* Gordon	Japanese Larch
Karin	*Chaenomeles sinensis* koehne.	Chinese Quince
Kashiwa	*Quercus dentata* Thunb.	Daimyo Oak
Kaya	*Torreya nucifera* Sieb. et Zucc.	Japanese Plum-Yew
Keyaki	*Zelkova serrata* Makino	Japanese Zelkova
Kobushi	*Magnolia kobus* DC.	Kobushi Magnolia
Kome-Tsuga	*Tsuga diversifolia* Mast.	Japanese Northern Hemlock
Konara	*Quercus serrata* Thunb.	Konara Oak, Small-Leaf Oak
Konote-Kashiwa	*Tsuja orientalis* L.	Chinese Arbor-vitae, Oriental Arbor-vitae
Kuchinashi	*Gardenia jasminoides* Ellis var. *grandiflora* Nakai	Cape Gardenia
Kuko	*Lycium chinense* Mill.	Fire Thorn, Box Thorn

(Japanese)	(Latin)	(English)
Kuma-Shide	*Carpinus carpinoides* Makino	Japanese Hornbeam
Kunugi	*Quercus actissima* Sieb. et Zucc.	Kunugi Oak, Chestnut-Leafed Oak
Kuri	*Castanea* spp.	Japanese Chestnut
Issai-Guri	*Castanea crenata* Sieb. et Zucc.	Chest tee 'Issai-Guri'
Kuro-Matsu	*Pinus thunbergii* Parl.	Japanese Black Pine
Nishiki-Matsu	*Pinus thunbergii* Parl.	Nishiki Pine
Kuro-Ezo-Matsu	*Picaea jezoensis* Carr.	Yesso Spruce
Mayumi	*Euonymus sieboldianus* Blume	Japanese Spindle Tree
Megi	*Berberis thunbergii* DC.	Japanese Barberry
Miyama Kirishima-	*Rhododendron kiusianum* Makino	Kirishima Azalea
Mokuren	*Magnolia liliflora* Desr.	Lily Magnolia
Momiji	*Acer palmatum* Thunb.	Maple
Iroha-Momiji, Iroha- Kaede, Takao- Momiji, 'Seigen'	*Acer palmatum* Thunb. var *palmatum*	Iroha-Maple, Iroha Kaede, Tkao Maple, 'Seigen'
Yama-Momiji	*Acer palmatum* Thunb. var. *matsumurae* Makino	Wild Maple
Nemu-no-ki	*Albizzia julibrissin* Durazz.	Silk Tree
Nire-Keyaki	*Zelkova serrata* Makino	Chinese Elm
Nishiki-gi	*Euonymus alata* Sieb.	Winged Spindle-Tree
No-Bara (No-lbara)	*Rosa multiflora* Thunb.	Japanese Dog Rose
Ōbai	*Jasminum nudiflorum* Lindl.	Winter Jasmine
Onkō (Ichii, Araragi)	*Taxus cuspidata* Sieb. et Zucc.	Japanese Yew
Rōbai	*Meratia praecox* Rehd. et Wilson	Winter Sweet, Bees-Wax Flower
Sakura	*Prunus* L.	Japanese Flowering Cherry
Yama-Zakura	*Prunus jamasakura* Sieb. et Zucc.	Japanese Hill Cherry
Sanzashi	*Crataegus cuneata* Sieb. et Zucc.	Nippon Hawthorn
Sarusuberi: Hyakujikko	*Lagerstroemia indica* L.	Crape Myrtle
Sasa	*Sasa* Makino	Small Bamboo
Satsuki	*Rhododendron lateritium* Planch.	Satsuki Azalea
Sawara	*Chamaecyparis pisifera* Sieb. et Zucc.	Sawara Cypress, Pea-fruited Cypress
Hime-Sawara	*Chamaecyparis pisifera* Endl.	
Sazanka	*Camellia sasanqua* Thunb.	Sasanqua Camellia
Shimpaku (Miyama Byakushin)	*Juniperus chinensis* L. var. *Sargentii* Henry	Chinese Juniper
Shirakaba	*Betula tanschii* Koidz.	Japanese White Birch
Soro (Shide)	*Carpinus laxiflora* Blume	Loose-Flowered Hornbeam
Sugi	*Cryptomeria japonica* D. Don	Japanese Cedar
Ma-Sugi	*Cryptomeria japonica* D. Don.	True Japanese Cedar
Tachibana-modoki	*Pyracantha augustifolia* Schneid.	Narrow-leaf Firethorn
Tō-Kaede	*Acer buergerianum* Miq.	Trident Maple
Toshō (Nezu)	*Juniperus rigida* Sieb. et Zucc.	Needle Juniper
Tsubaki	*Camellia japonica* L.	Garden Camellia
Tsuta	*Parthenocissus tricuspidata* Planch.	Japanese Ivy, Boston Ivy
Tsutsuji	*Rhododendron* spp.	Azarea
Kishi-Tsutsuji	*Rhododendron ripense* Makino	Kishi Tsutsuji
Ume	*Prunus mume* Sieb. et Zucc.	Japanese Flowering Apricot
Shidare	"	Drooping Japanese Apricot
Ume-modoki	*Irex Serrata* var. Sieboldii Losen.	Finetooth Holly
Yanagi	*Salix* L.	Weeping Willow
Yusura-Ume	*Prunus Tomentosa* Thunb.	Tomentose Cherry
Yore-Nezu	*Juni[eris rigida* var. *filiformis* Mixim	Needle-Juniper, Stiff-leaved Juniper
Zaifuri-boku	*Amelanchier asiatica* Endl.	Japanese Juneberry
Zakuro	*Punica granatum* L.	Common Pomegranate

INDEX

Photo credit:
P. 5, 20, 25
  Shin Kikaku Co., Ltd.
P. 103
  Kindai Shuppan Co., Ltd.